INFANT
EDUCATION

INFANT EDUCATION:
A Guide for Helping Handicapped Children in the First Three Years

edited by
Bettye M. Caldwell
and Donald J. Stedman
in association with
Kennith W. Goin

Published by

 Walker and Company
720 Fifth Avenue
New York, NY 10019

for

The Technical Assistance Development System
A Division of Frank Porter Graham
Child Development Center at
The University of North Carolina, Chapel Hill

Acknowledgments

Many people have helped create this manuscript. In addition to the authors, editors, and production staff, we are especially grateful to those persons from the various First Chance Projects who attended the TADS' Conference on Infant Education in San Antonio. They supported and enriched this book. In particular we would like to acknowledge the assistance of William Gingold, Thomas Clark, Claire Salant, Wanda Elder, Martha Moersch, and Diana Pefley whose reactions were very helpful in developing the final manuscript.

This book was developed pursuant to a grant from the United States Office of Education. Points of view or opinions expressed herein do not necessarily represent official Office of Education positions or policy.

First published in the United States of America in 1977 by the Walker Publishing Company, Inc.

Published simultaneously in Canada by Fitzhenry & Whiteside, Limited, Toronto

Cloth ISBN: 0-8027-9042-9

Paper ISBN: 0-8027-7110-6

Library of Congress Catalog Card Number: 76-52245

Printed in the United States of America

10 9 8 7 6 5 4 3 2 1

Contents

Acknowledgments iv

Foreword vii

CHAPTER 1 Early Childhood Intervention Programs
Donald J. Stedman 1

CHAPTER 2 Early Detection of Children with
   Handicapping Conditions: Implications for Educators
William K. Frankenburg 13

CHAPTER 3 Infant Assessment
   and Developmental Handicaps
Rune J. Simeonsson 27

CHAPTER 4 The Infant Stimulation/Mother
   Training Project
Earladeen Badger 45

CHAPTER 5 Preventing Mental Retardation
   Through Family Rehabilitation
Howard L. Garber 63

CHAPTER 6 The Children's Center and the Family
   Development Research Program
Alice S. Honig 81

CHAPTER 7 An Introduction to the Carolina
   Abecedarian Project
Craig T. Ramey, Margaret C. Holmberg,
Joseph H. Sparling, and Albert M. Collier **101**

CHAPTER 8 Intervention Programs for Children
   Under Three Years
M. H. Jones **123**

CHAPTER 9 Evaluating Program Effectiveness
Bettye M. Caldwell **147**

Index **161**

Foreword

The period of eighteen months to three years appears to be the time at which significant developmental differences in children from relatively privileged and underprivileged backgrounds begin to surface. This finding has suggested to many educators, psychologists, and other child care providers that "infancy" is the best time to begin working with children who are disadvantaged either because of their environment or because of medical or psychological handicaps. This book examines some of the remarkable work that has been done with infants in this country in the past few years.

In 1975, several recognized infant educators were asked to write papers on their work (which in some cases spanned more than two-and-one-half decades) with handicapped children under three. These papers, which were presented to a conference of infant educators from the First Chance Network (San Antonio), addressed the practical problems encountered in administering programs for infants. The nine chapters of this book are the end result of the San Antonio presentations.

Chapter 1 contains a discussion of the present state of our knowledge about the effects, both positive and negative, of existing programs for infants. Chapters 2 and 3 include information on certain screening and assessment procedures which have been successfully used with children between the ages of zero and three. Chapters 4 through 8 are essentially case studies of highly successful, well known infant programs. Chapter 9 is an examination of the issues involved in evaluating the effectiveness of programs for preschool handicapped children.

We at TADS are pleased to have had an opportunity to participate in the development of this book. We feel sure that it will prove an asset to those who are dedicated to working with handicapped infants and preschoolers.

CHAPTER *1*

Early Childhood Intervention Programs

Donald J. Stedman

In 1972, Secretary of Health, Education and Welfare Elliott Richardson commissioned five educators[1] to review the effectiveness of "early education intervention" programs. One of the principal concerns which prompted the study was the apparent difficulty of moving small, successful, research programs into more widespread practice, a typical problem in American education. Special focus, consequently, was placed on projects addressing high risk, preschool-aged children. The review included a close examination of the research literature, on-site visits to highly recommended projects, and extensive interviews with fourteen competent and respected researchers in the field.

The results of the survey were significant because they indicated, rather clearly, that educational programs for preschool, handicapped children—whether they be infants or five-year-olds—*can* significantly improve the quality of the children's lives.

In this chapter, the evidence which supports intervention, as well as certain problems with present intervention programs, will be discussed.

[1] The five were the author, and Dr. Ira Gordon, University of Florida; Dr. Ron Parker, Random House; Dr. Paul Dokecki, George Peabody College; and Dr. Nicholas Anastasiow, University of Indiana. The study was conducted under contract HEWOOS-72-205.

DONALD J. STEDMAN is Associate Director of the Frank Porter Graham Child Development Center and Professor of Education at the University of North Carolina. His professional interests include child development and mental retardation.

1

IN SUPPORT OF INTERVENTION

The Findings

The results of a close examination of more than forty longitudinal intervention research programs for high risk children included the following major findings:

1. The manner in which a child is reared and the environment into which he is born have a major impact on what he will become.

2. Factors such as race and sex do not appear to be related to the child's ability to profit from intervention programs.

3. The family's methods of establishing social roles leave little doubt that early family environment (parental language styles, attitudes toward achievement, parental involvement and concern for the child) has a significant impact on the child's development before he reaches his second birthday.

4. In situations where families are so disorganized that they cannot supply a supportive environment, an intensive external supportive environment may contribute to the child's development.

5. The effects of a stimulating or depriving environment appear to be most powerful in the early years of childhood when the most rapid growth and development take place. The primary locus of the child during these early years is the home. Therefore, home-based intervention programs or one-to-one teacher-child ratio stimulation activities appear to be the most appropriate and effective during this period.

6. There is evidence that the effects of early intervention programs for children are strengthened by the involvement of the child's parents.

7. It is only possible to describe the training conditions that handicap a child or lead to a child's success in general terms.

8. The socio-economic status and entry level IQ of the child bear an uncertain relationship to the child's ability to profit from intervention. Design problems and the current state of the art in

measurement render the effect of these factors difficult to determine.

9. Where access to children can be gained in the early years, preferably during the language emergent years (one to two years of age), intervention programs will be more effective than those begun at later ages.

10. A systematic organized program can contribute significantly to a child's social and intellectual development between the ages of four and six years.

11. The effects of intervention programs appear to last only so long as the child remains in the intervention program. They appear to last longer in home training studies and "wash out" sooner in school programs.

12. Follow-up studies of children in intervention programs usually show that initial gains are no longer measurable. This is partially attributable to the fact that we cannot determine at this point whether it is due to program failure, to problems of measurement, to inadequate criterion measures, or to the later interfering effects of other competing environments, such as the home and school.

13. The quality and motivation of the staff are directly related to the success of the program and therefore are prime factors in determining the extent to which a program is exportable or replicable.

Successful Intervention

Some findings are worthy of special note since they concern frequently asked but seldom answered questions of importance to researchers and educational practitioners:

In the successful programs, gains occur regardless of age of entry. The starting age of children placed in intervention programs has varied across projects from those starting at a few months of age to a beginning age of five or six years. Results reported by at least one study have shown that children who enter learning-to-learn programs at age four make gains of nearly 20 IQ points which are maintained during the following two years. Children who enter at age five make smaller gains for each of the two years (9 points the first year and 7 points the second year). Although these results suggest differential gains as a function of age of entry, they do not answer the correlated question of whether gains would be sustained after the first year in the absence of such a program.

However, data from another project indicate that children who made gains in the project when they entered did not lose those gains as long as they remained in the program. The data do not strongly support any one year as the more preferred year to realize gains in intellectual growth.

Hence, the general conclusion must be that programs have been effective with all ages and one cannot specifically support the advantages for work at any one year versus another.

None of the studies reviewed gives support to a well defined critical period as a preference for preschool or early childhood intervention. Essentially, programs can be designed that will work effectively with a wide age range.

A comprehensive review of intervention programs in 1970 suggested that vulnerability to adverse influences at certain ages does not necessarily imply a correlated time when children are especially sensitive to treatment. This study supported the contention that, on the basis of our current level of knowledge, intervention can be justified throughout the period of early development and possibly beyond.

In successful programs, gains occur regardless of sex. While studies have reported that girls have higher initial IQs than boys, gains were not related to the sex of the child. These findings are supported in general by other investigators, many of whom do not separate IQ scores by sex when reporting gains because of the lack of differences.

In successful programs, gains occur regardless of race. Studies again report that although whites enter with higher initial IQ scores, race is not a significant variable in considering gain scores.

Differential gains in IQ scores occur as a function of the entering or initial IQ score, the program intensity, and the duration or length of time a child is in the program. In general, the lower the initial IQ, the greater the gain in IQ in the intervention program. Again, the more intense the program, the more likely he is to have a higher IQ gain. Finally, the interaction between intensity of program and duration in program contributes to differential gains. Some researchers, Bronfenbrenner for example, attribute the high initial gains to the phenomenon of *regression to the mean* and characterize the gains as being *inflated* for that reason.

In successful programs, gains occur regardless of program approach but some programs appear to be better than others. Although almost all kinds of programs have shown gains in IQ scores, some differences are evident, when specific comparisons are made among programs. In general, it should be stated that some programs work while others do not. In those that are successful, it is apparent that the degree of program structuring is higher than that of unsuccessful programs. In general, the more structure, the greater the gain of IQ in participating children. A large-scale comparison among programs has been conducted by using four groups (regular nursery school, children from low income families in middle class nursery groups, Montessori or perceptual motor skill groups, and an experimental group with a highly structured format). When gain scores on the *Stanford-Binet* were compared, the experimental group (the structured) program was perceived as having the largest gains. It should be mentioned that the experimental group emphasized verbal behavior, a procedure which would tend to influence test scores. Although the remaining three groups may have excelled on other measures, the program of the experimental group resulted in the largest gain on intelligence test scores (IQs).

THE PROBLEMS WITH PRESENT INTERVENTION EFFORTS

A number of serious cautions, which emerge from the review and consideration of research and development activity in this area, involve the scope of present efforts.

1. The sample size of most projects is insufficient for the amount of trust and credibility placed on their outcomes.

2. There is insufficient research in the area to date. After ten years, the number of well-designed and well-executed studies still number less than forty.

3. The majority of studies do not involve the subjects in the intervention program for a sufficient amount of time to allow for long-term change or an adequate test of the intervention program.

4. Insufficient attention is paid to the effects of mixing varieties of children, handicapped and non-handicapped, in order to improve the learning environment in which the intervention program is taking place.

5. The current measures available to assess change in children as a result of intervention program effects are inadequate in number

and quality.

6. The low utility and low reliability of pre-test scores from high risk children (resulting from their meager amount of experience with testing or evaluation approaches) may lead us to infer greater gains from post-test scores than should be inferred as resulting from intervention activities.

7. There is increasing doubt as to the value of certain critical periods; therefore, the extent to which we can continue to emphasize only one period when we can expect positive outcomes of early intervention activities to occur is questionable.

8. There is a typical failure to individualize programs. That is, there is a homogeneity of treatment whether it be social class, IQ level, sex, minority group, or other critical features, across heterogeneous groups.

9. There are often significant cultural differences among minority and ethnic groups leading to differential reactions to intervention programs. This may lead to exaggerated responses from the children in either direction. Also, there are in many cases extreme value differences between subjects and their families and the project staff which may lead to inadequate or inappropriate intervention program components and results.

10. Program goals are often too narrow and constricted. There is more to development than IQ.

11. There are certain gains or responses to the intervention activities which are related to the motivation of the parents to encourage and assist their child in participating in the program. This parental support factor is not often considered as a part of what accounts for intervention programs' success.

12. There are severe logistical problems in connection with both the conduct of longitudinal studies and the development of exportable intervention program components.

13. There is an insufficient number of replications of special studies showing positive or hopeful results.

14. The cost of longitudinal studies has resulted in too few compre-

hensive studies, including health, education, social, and parent program components.

In general, the group concluded that preschool educational intervention programs *do* have important and positive effects on the *IQ* of children. The results are often uneven and transient. There has not yet been sufficient research to warrant the selection of one specific set of program components as being the most contributive to cognitive and social gains.

Special Problems

A number of obstacles in conducting studies appear to be adding to the difficulty of determining the effectiveness and credibility of outcomes.

Inadequate control groups Given the problem of adequately describing the population, it rarely becomes possible to determine the adequacy of the control group. Rarely are children selected from the same population pool and randomly assigned to treatment groups.

Treatment drift Once an evaluation model is adopted, decisions are made to change the program according to information gathered. This is a highly acceptable practice in the remediation of children's deficiencies. As this occurs, however, the intervention program is no longer being conducted as originally described. As a longitudinal study refines its procedures, new strategies are invented; thus the original procedures are markedly changed. Frequently, the change is not described in the write-up.

Press to do well Most innovators are funded to demonstrate the effectiveness of a given idea or program. They are expected to succeed. Given the press to succeed, the program is constantly revised and modified on the basis of pupil responses. In a process similar to that of treatment drift, the program in operation often bears little resemblance to the written proposal.

Teacher effect Evidence indicates that the teacher, not the program, may be the crucial variable in creating change. Indications are that the method or program adopted interacts with the stylistic treatment of the teacher. Teacher factors relating to the change are highly idiosyncratic and difficult to control. One researcher has identified four major clusters of teachers on the basis of control and expressions of warmth. Another researcher has pursued other sets of teacher personality factors that influence pupil change. Yet another has identified planning and supervision as being more important to the program than the curriculum components themselves. How you do something may be more important than what you do.

Teachers reach criterion performance Frequently, a program is developed by an innovator who then hires a staff to conduct the program. In the experience of the author, it frequently take as long as two to three years before the staff can conduct the program as originally conceived. Massive in-service efforts with frequent supervision and evaluation of teacher performance, are needed in all intervention programs. Some personnel will not be able to reach criterion performance and will need to be replaced.

Ethics with human subjects The innovator, in dealing with human subjects, cannot manipulate the research environment unless he is sure he will not damage the child in any way. This ethical "restriction" is necessary in working with human subjects and limits the degree of manipulation the innovator can apply. For example, does one remove children from their mothers in order to work intensively with them?

Continuity of staffing As with life-span research projects, it is difficult for a principal investigator to commit himself over his own life span. If the principal investigator leaves the project, there may be a shift in focus or interest when a new principal investigator takes over. There are also changes in staff training or staff development activities and staff turnover, especially in university-based programs where graduate students are used extensively.

Testing procedures Again, as with life-span research projects, testing schedules, instrument revision, and discontinuity and low correlation between tests brought into the long-term testing activity make conducting the project and interpreting the data difficult.

Data processing Masses of data, which may accumulate in longitudinal studies, can present both problems of data processing and difficulties in decision making as to which data to process. This data accumulation is especially problematic for the new researcher in the intervention field.

Environmental changes Children in longitudinal studies are often influenced by major shifts in the community or neighborhood environment. These shifts may have a direct effect on the outcome of the intervention activities. Shifts in cultural mores, social attitudes, and values may have similar effects.

Attrition The mobility of the American family is well known. While techniques are available to adjust to subject attrition, it is an expensive process and often requires resources not provided in the intervention programs. It is essential that large subject samples be acquired and maintained over a long period of time in order to circumvent the problems caused by subject attrition.

Interpretation

Often, the interpretation of the results of well designed and conducted studies constitutes a major task. The group attempted to examine the nature of interpretation problems and suggested the following points:

Nature of the population In work with high risk youngsters, the set of variables associated is multiple and often incomparable. For example, the construct "culturally deprived," used by different research workers, includes: income level, racial differences, inadequate diet, protein deficiency, punitive child-rearing practices, low language stimulation, isolation, oppression, high disease rates, alcoholism, and so on. It often is assumed that all of these factors contribute the same influence. Clearly, the state of the art—when it comes to knowledge of how to deal effectively with high risk populations—it is not developed to the point at which the population of children can be described with the precision needed to replicate a study. In addition children who live in poverty are still found in markedly different environments—for example, contrast the immigrant worker's child with the child of the inner city dweller or the sharecropper. The life experiences are markedly different.

Problems of program description One of the major problems in interpreting intervention programs is that often the program descriptions are not sufficiently detailed to make clear what it was that the innovator did. Global terms that make it difficult either to replicate or to isolate the variables that were related to the treatment are frequently used. For example, a study of adopted versus non-adopted children may not adequately define the nature of the treatment, i.e., what happened in the homes that did not happen in the orphanages to cause the results. Longitudinal intervention studies rarely describe all of the procedures used in beginning and maintaining a program. It is, in fact, frequently impossible to describe exactly what was done in a program. A major intervention program may have components that deal with classroom experiences, parent training, improved nutrition, medical screening, and vision and hearing tests. Ascribing treatment success to any one variable is a tenuous procedure.

Failure to develop appropriate instruments One of the major difficulties in conducting studies with children is specifying exactly what evaluation the innovator will be able to perform after the intervention. Many programs specify IQ scores as their objective. However, IQ scores are unreliable and invalid for most minority group children and, moreover, IQ refers more to traits related to school performance than to cognitive functioning. The appeal of the behaviorally oriented programs is their tendency to limit their goals to observable behaviors. However, the weakness of this approach is that one is still left with the problem of defining the "internal processes" of the child and, frequently, minor and sometimes irrelevant behaviors.

Global measures of intelligence and achievement are inappropriate measures for program impact. Intelligence measures assume common cultural experiences, equal opportunity to learn, and equal motivation to do well on the tests. For most minority group children, these assumptions cannot be met.

Achievement tests contain many items aimed at reasoning ability rather than at the skill under treatment. For example, as much as fifty percent of elementary school reading tests are inference problems rather than reading problems. Reading is learning a set of abstract arbitrary symbols and relating them to another set of symbols that are spoken—that is speech. Children can relate words to print and learn that the printed word stands for the spoken word or for objects, but unless long trials of memorization, drill, and practice techniques are used, children do not understand the abstraction of graphemics until ten to twelve years of age. Thus, many reading tests are misnamed; they would be more appropriately titled "reading from reading" tests.

Intuitive appeal of gain scores In spite of the work of Cronbach, Thorndike, and others who demonstrated that gain scores are unreliable, statistically indefensible, and subject to great misinterpretation for individuals or groups, there still exists great pressure for programs to demonstrate effectiveness by measuring gains on the same instrument.

Measurement should not concern itself with change as measured by gain scores but with change measured by performance of the desired behavior that defines the criterion performance. Criterion-referenced tests are difficult to construct unless the behaviors are readily observable. For example, it is easier to specify that, as a result of the program, children will be able to count to ten or identify six primary colors than to specify that they will develop a positive self-concept and attitude towards others.

Inadequate or naive theory of human behavior Many longitudinal studies fail to conceptualize the nature of human learning and the processes of development. The results of these studies can easily be misinterpreted. Recent findings in developmental theory and learning have been massive. The human organism is an impressive information processor from the moment of birth. Many, however, still failing to recognize the infant's capacity to process information continue to perceive the child as a passive receptor of information, and thereby attribute to their training procedures more power than is likely to be present. In the same way, the innovator who works with the handicapped child frequently views all that the child lacks in terms of and as a function of his handicap without taking into account his age and the normal stages of growth and development.

Retrospective data, time, and cost Most retrospective data collected from teachers and parents bear little resemblance to the child's actual functioning. The unreliability of these data makes longitudinal studies all the more necessary. However, longitudinal studies take time and careful record keeping. It may be twenty years before the effects of the intervention program can be fully measured. Longitudinal studies are costly ventures, although they may be the only means by which some questions can be answered.

Delayed effects Rarely do longitudinal studies measure delayed effects of their treatment. For example, does the program introduced in kindergarten have any measurable effects on adolescent behavior? Rarely do school programs measure adult attitudes, voting habits, reading habits, or other goals which were part of the school curriculum.

Narrow focus of the program Some longitudinal studies become so specialized and deal with such a narrow population that they cannot be replicated. For example, a program that provides a one-to-one teacher/pupil ratio for six hours a day, six days a week, with supporting psychological, medical, and speech staff would be difficult to find in a regular school.

Sample problems The size of the sample and the representativeness of the sample must be taken into account more seriously. Samples have generally been too small to allow for much generalization. The results of a program that also limits itself to a unique population have little generalizability to other populations of high risk children. Further, shrinkage of already small samples occurs over time and contributes to the lack of follow-up results or effects.

The effect of continued assessment or observation The effects of continuous testing in long-term studies, including observer effects, can have an equal or perhaps greater effect on performance than some or all of the program components. In many programs, continuous assessment and the intervention curriculum are confounded in such a way as to prevent attribution of responsibility for changes in a child to either assessment or curriculum. In some cases, continuous assessment of control groups may contribute to changes that are equal to changes in the experimental group and thereby make it impossible to measure the effect of the intervention program itself. In some cases, researchers suggest that continuous assessment is equivalent to minimal intervention. Intervention studies are no less immune to the Hawthorne effect than other studies.

SUMMARY

In the final analysis, even given the cautions, design problems, and difficulites with data interpretation, it was felt that we already know a great deal about the effectiveness of educational intervention. In general, there are positive effects. A host of factors, including child variables, setting variables, and the characteristics of the intervention program and the people delivering it, operate to make education more or less effective for the individual child.

More research is required, in the field with carefully described curriculum components and the best child variable control possible, within bounds of natural groupings of children. If there is a prime obstacle, it is lack of measurement tools for social, affective, and interpersonal change, as well as for academic gain. Methods of coding and analyzing observational data lag far behind other methods in the social sciences.

Finally, the expensive, long-term, longitudinal study of development in children is still the best strategy for discovering environmental effects. The major difficulty is getting public or private resources to support these operations.

CHAPTER 2

Early Detection of Children with Handicapping Conditions: Implications for Educators

William K. Frankenburg

INTRODUCTION

Before one can treat or educate a handicapped child who would other-wise, in later years, be destined to fail in school, it is necessary to identify the child. This chapter addresses itself to the rationale for early identifica-tion; the general process by which such children are identified; specific techniques employed to screen, diagnose, and treat handicapping condi-tions; and the planning of a community early identification and treat-ment program.

RATIONALE FOR EARLY IDENTIFICATION

A number of studies have amply demonstrated the importance of the first few years of life and the manner in which they set the stage for later development. Specialists in the field of special education, speech pathol-ogy, psychology, and pediatrics have also demonstrated that the earlier some of these handicapping conditions are corrected, the less will be the permanent handicap. This observation is particularly true for the critical first three years of life when the brain is growing very rapidly and the child

---

WILLIAM K. FRANKENBURG is an Associate Professor of Pediatrics at the University of Colorado Medical Center in Denver. One of his primary interests is screening programs for young children.

is making his most rapid advances in development. Although many types of handicapping conditions (such as Down's Syndrome and severe mental retardation) are readily apparent, a far greater number of children have handicaps of a lesser magnitude which, though still requiring early detection and treatment, are not so apparent. The identification of these children is based upon two processes: the first is screening, and the second is diagnosis.

Screening is the presumptive identification of unrecognized disease or defects by the application of tests, examinations, or other procedures which can be applied rapidly and economically to large populations of people. Screening serves to sort out the apparently well from those who are very probably not well. The individuals who, when screened, are suspect, require a subsequently more detailed evaluation to establish the diagnosis. The purpose of screening is to move up the time of diagnosis in the disease process to a time that precedes the usual time of diagnosis. To justify the extra effort and cost involved in screening, conditions screened for must meet most of the following criteria:

1. The condition being screened for benefits from treatment.

2. Early treatment (as a result of screening) improves the prognosis more than treatment at the usual time of diagnosis.

3. The condition can be diagnosed through the application of diagnostic tests.

4. Facilities for diagnosis and treatment are available.

5. The condition is relatively prevalent.

6. Suitable tests or procedures to screen for the condition are available.

   a. These tests are accurate in identifying most of the individuals with the problem and miss few individuals who have the problem. In addition, most of the individuals who, on screening, are suspect, will be diagnosed as having the problem (there are few over-referrals).
   b. The test is rapid.
   c. The test is economical.
   d. The test uses minimal, if any professional time.
   e. The test is acceptable to professional persons who perform

the diagnostic follow-up of children with suspect screening results.

f.   The test is acceptable to the public.

Screening tests do not make a diagnosis. It would be incorrect to make a diagnosis or to plan a treatment program solely on the basis of screening results. This point cannot be emphasized too strongly, for far too often people equate screening results with diagnostic results. Screening is only *presumptive* identification.

In this author's opinion, a number of large scale screening programs have been abandoned after the expenditure of much time, money, and effort. Had the preceding criteria been considered prior to screening, the unprofitable screening may not have been undertaken. Some examples of screening programs that have been tried and generally abandoned are: newborn auditory screening with the Warblet—the Warblet lacked sufficient accuracy in identifying all of the infants with congenital hearing loss; sickle cell screening—diagnosis did not improve the prognosis; biochemical laboratory screening for ten or more problems—the screening procedure was not accurate enough in identifying the diseased subjects; streptococcal screening—the small benefits in the prevention of complications such as rheumatic fever did not justify the cost because of the low prevalence of rheumatic fever and the cost of treating the many asymptomatic carriers who would never develop the complications but might develop penicillin sensitivity reactions.

In addition, there are a number of conditions which, although presently being screened for, are of dubious value. Some of these are: screening for perceptual problems—since the diagnostic tests are not sufficiently defined to determine which child will benefit from treatment and which will not; and screening for eye motor coordination "problems" since there are no scientific studies that children exhibiting such so-called problems are destined to suffer from school learning disorders.

Diagnostic tests and procedures are generally administered and interpreted by specialists such as psychologists, physicians, speech pathologists, audiologists, etc. Their diagnoses are most often based upon a history of the evolution of the problem, a family history to determine if other family members had similar or related problems, and a detailed evaluation that may consist of the application of tests, such as auditory testing in a sound proofed room and otoscopic examination of the ears. Such evaluations are more time consuming and thorough than are screening tests. The cost of such evaluations is considerably higher than that of screening procedures because of the larger amount of professional time involved and the use of more expensive equipment. Such diagnostic procedures generally result in a diagnosis, a measure of the extent of impairment, and possibly a prescription for treatment.

Treatment, as referred to in this chapter, pertains to a prescription (as for glasses), a hearing aid, or medications. The prescription may also consist of therapy (such as physical therapy) or speech therapy. The prescription is almost always made by the professional person who also made the diagnosis.

The educational assessment or prescription is most often evolved by an educator, or in some cases by a psychologist. Such assessments may be partially based upon tests, but for the most part they are based upon the child's areas of strength and weakness, as well as upon observations of how the child learns. Such evaluations are carried out over an extended period of time and are an ongoing process. The educational assessment is primarily performed in the classroom. Not all handicapped children require an educational program. For instance, a child not exhibiting delays in development may only require a pair of glasses. Another child who is visually handicapped may be delayed in his cognitive development and require not only glasses but remedial education. Children primarily requiring special educational assistance are those that have been delayed in their development or those for whom delayed development is anticipated at a subsequent time.

It is necessary that educators working with handicapped children have a basic understanding of screening procedures and what is entailed in diagnosis and treatment. Since this book addresses itself to children below three years of age, the identification of children with visual. audial, and developmental handicaps will be discussed. Emotional problems are generally difficult to diagnose before three years of age and, therefore, will not be discussed. Severe emotional problems, such as autism and extreme withdrawal, will generally be identified through developmental screening. Screening procedures for child abuse and environmental deprivation will not be discussed, even though they are important, because valid procedures are still being developed. Screening for medical disorders such as phenylketonuria, galactosemia, blood incompatibility, genetic disorders, etc., is also not discussed because treatment has primarily medical implications.

SCREENING, DIAGNOSIS AND TREATMENT OF HEARING DISORDERS AND MIDDLE EAR DISEASE.

The purpose of auditory screening is to identify children whose hearing is reduced enough to interfere with their social and educational contacts and responses. Normal hearing, particularily during the first years of life, is essential to learning. It is, perhaps, the most important avenue of learning since, without the perception of sound, one cannot learn speech. Speech is required for communication and for learning about one's environment. A hearing impairment, particularily during the first few years of life, may interfere with normal intellectual development. The prevalence of congenital hearing loss is about 1 in 1,000, whereas the prevalence of conductive hearing loss during the first three years of life is approximately 30 percent. The figure generally varies with the economic status of the family and is more common among children of low income families. Ideally, all children should be screened at birth and at six, twelve, eighteen, twenty-four and thirty-six months of age. Thereafter, less frequent screening is required. The following procedure is recommended in the **Guide to Screening EPSDT Medicaid** children:

Method of Screening

a) *Birth* It is recommended that newborns be evaluated with a medical history and a physical examination which notes: 1) family history of hereditary childhood hearing impairment; 2) rubella or other nonbacterial intrauterine fetal infection (e.g., cytomegalvirus infections, Herpes infection); 3) defects of ear, nose, or throat such as malformed (low-set or absent) pinnae, cleft lip or palate (including submucous cleft), or any other abnormality of the otorhinolaryngeal system; 4) birthweight below 1500 grams; 5) serum bilirubin greater than 20 mg./100 ml.; and 6) bacterial meningitis. Any newborn who manifests any of these abnormalitties is considered to be positive or suspect. Such infants should be tested audiologically within two or three months after birth and retested at intervals thereafter. Auditory testing of babies in the newborn nursery is not currently recommended except for purposes of research.

b) *Six months through twenty-four months* It is recommended that an infant's ability to hear and to respond verbally be evaluated by utilizing the series of parent-answered questions presented in Appendix A. The infant's failure to make all of the auditory responses appropriate for his age constitutes a positive response and he should be rescreened a month later. If the response is still positive, the child should be referred to an audiologist. If possible, the infant's ability to hear should also be ascertained during this age period through the use of calibrated noisemakers.

c) *Three years of age* It is recommended that children three years of age be evaluated by using pure-tone audiometry testing of each ear at 1,000, 2,000, and 4,000 Hz at 15 dB ANSI if the ambient (environmental) noise level is low enough. If the ambient noise level is not very low, testing at 25 dB is recommended. A positive response is a failure to respond to the 15 or 25 dB tone at any two frequencies with either or both ears. Some three-year-olds may require play-conditioning audiometry to determine whether or not they hear the auditory signals.

Diagnostic Evaluation

Newborns with a history suggesting the likelihood of deafness should, in addition to receiving necessary medical supervision, be futher evaluated by an audiologist in a soundproof room at four, eight, and twelve months to rule out a hearing loss.

Whereas pure-tone audiometry is designed to detect the presence of hearing loss through measurement of sensitivity to sound, assessing the auditory function by using an acoustic impedance bridge is an electroacoustic measurement of the compliance of the middle ear system. It is an objective measure of the conducting system and does not require a voluntary response from the patient. This technique is, therefore, ideally suited for screening infants. The chief drawback of this simple, quick screening procedure is the initial cost of the equipment which varies from $2,000 to $2,800.

SCREENING, DIAGNOSIS AND TREATMENT OF EYE DISORDERS

The primary objective in eye screening of children is to detect potentially blinding diseases and visual impairments which will interfere with the development and education of the child. Two-thirds of the eye problems detected are refractive errors that may be detected with visual acuity screening. Muscle imbalance and amblyopia are far less frequent, and other problems such as glaucoma, tumors, ocular infections, and injuries are relatively rare. Amblyopia or "Lazy Eye" is loss of vision resulting from disuse of an eye. Such disuse may be due to the child seeing double (because one eye is turned in, out, up, or down) or due to a marked difference in visual acuity between the two eyes. The prevalence of these eye problems in children below three years of age is not known but is thought to affect possibly five percent of the population. It is important to identify such eye problems as early as possible in the life of the child because most of these conditions progress if not treated, and the later treatment is begun, the worse the ultimate prognosis. All children should be screened at birth, at six and twelve months, and every two to three years thereafter.

Method of Screening

a) *Birth through one year*
   1) General external examination and evaluation of ocular motility.
   2) Gross visual acuity examination with fixation test.
   3) Testing light sense with pupillary light reflex test.
   4) Intraocular examination with ophthalmoscope.

b) *Two and three years*
   1) Visual acuity testing. Visual acuity for distance should be tested separately for each eye. Tests which may be employed are the STYCAR (Screening Test of Young Children and Retardates) and the Allen picture-card tests. Children from two to five years of age should be tested at ten or fifteen feet.

Pass-fail criteria vary in different screening programs. Most people agree that three-year-old children who demonstrate a visual acuity of less than 20/40 in either eye or who demonstrate a one-line difference in visual acuity between the two eyes within the passing range deserve further evaluation.

   2) *Muscle imbalance* The parent should be asked whether the child's eyes ever turn in or out. The alternate cover test of the Hirschberg test (corneal light reflex) should be given. A parent's report that a child's eyes turn in or out, or a deviation of one of the eyes as revealed by the alternate cover test or the Hirschberg test, are generally considered to be positive findings.

   3) *Other* A general inspection of the eyes should be performed. Evidence of infection, congenital abnormalities, the presence of redness, discharge, enlarged or hazy cornea, obvious deviation of eye, excessive blinking, squinting, and congested lids should all be considered as positive findings.

Children who wear glasses should be tested while wearing their glasses. If acuity is "normal" while glasses are worn, annual checkups should be recommended to ensure that acuity does not change and that glasses fit. If acuity while glasses are worn is abnormal, futher evaluation is required unless a recent examination has ensured that the best possible correction has been achieved. Children who fail the initial screening test should be rescreened on another day to be sure that the abnormal test was not due to temporary factors in the child or the testing environment. Children failing the second screening may be referred directly to an eye specialist or seen by their physician and then by a specialist. Test results should be interpreted to the parents, and the importance of an eye examination for those who have failed should be stressed. It is important to provide the referral specialist with the results of the screening test and to request a report of the specialist's findings. Follow-up efforts with the parents should continue until children obtain the recommended eye examination and the necessary correction or treatment. Children whose central vision is not sufficiently improved by lenses to pass the screening test obviously require a diagnostic evaluation.

Children who are suspect on the eye screening procedures require a complete eye examination by an ophthalmologist or an optometrist. The former is a physician. Either will apply a series of diagnostic tests to determine if the child in question actually has an eye problem.

SCREENING, DIAGNOSIS, AND TREATMENT OF CHILDREN WITH DEVELOPMENTAL PROBLEMS

The aim of developmental screening is to identify children who have significant deviations in psychological, neurological, or emotional development. Many causes of delayed development are amenable to treatment if detected early. Early identification is particularily important since development proceeds at such a rapid rate during the first three years of life. Furthermore, the children who lack adequate environmental support begin to show a deceleration in development as early as eighteen months of age. Delays in detection beyond that age, therefore, cause these children to receive treatment only after they have shown developmental lags. The prevalence of developmental disabilities in the population varies with the definition of what constitutes such a problem and with population characteristics such as economic status.

Since developmental delays may develop at any time in the life of the child, the earlier treatment is initiated, the better. Since development proceeds at a very rapid rate during the first three years of life, periodic screening should be performed several times during the first year of life and less often during the following years. It is recommended that all children be screened at three, six, nine, twelve, eighteen, twenty-four, and thirty-six months of life. Such screening can be accomplished through use of a two-stage screening procedure. The first stage consists of a simple developmental questionnaire that a parent answers at the previously indicated ages of the child. Children who are suspect as a result of parental responses on the questionnaire undergo a second stage of screening with a longer, more accurate, developmental screening test to reduce the over-referrals.

Method of Screening

Two screening questionnaires are ideally suited to the first stage of screening since each is designed to be used for prescreening and to be followed with a more accurate and complicated screening test. The first is the Denver Prescreening Developmental Questionnaire (PDQ) which is designed for use in conjunction with the Denver Developmental Screening Test (DDST). An alternate is to use the Developmental Screening Inventory Questionnaire, which is designed for use with the Developmental Screening Inventory (DSI). Whereas the DDST and its questionnaire cover the age range from birth to six years, the DSI and its questionnaire cover the age range from birth to three years. Though many other developmental screening questionnaires are available, most have not been validated.

Diagnostic Evaluation

It is recommended that all children who are positive on the questionnaire be screened with one of the screening tests named prior to referral for a diagnostic evaluation. The only economical exception to this procedure might be the child who passes almost none of the questions appropriate for his age and who shows obvious signs of being developmentally delayed. A complete medical and thorough social history should be taken for children who, on the basis of the screening test, are found to be questionable, borderline or abnormal. Special emphasis should be placed on questions related to causes of developmental delays (complications of pregnancy, illnesses such as meningitis, deprivation, etc.). Each child should also receive thorough physical and neurological evaluations. Diagnostic examination with tests such as the Revised Bayley Scale of Infant Development, the Stanford-Binet, or the Gesell examination will serve to establish the child's current developmental level and areas of strength and weakness in his performance. Such evaluations should be performed by a psychologist or a pediatrician who has had extensive experience in evaluating children who are three and fewer years of age. This is an important consideration since many psychologists have little if any experience in evaluating infants. An audiological or ophthalmological examination may also be indicated to rule out delays in development that are due to sensory defects. Laboratory tests such as phenylalanine levels, thyroid function tests, or an EEG may be indicated if a metabolic disorder or seizures are suspected.

Upon the establishment of the diagnosis and the child's level of function, specific medical treatment (medication, diet, or physical therapy, etc.) may be prescribed. Consideration should also be given to educational opportunities in the form of center-based or home-based programs. As a child is enrolled in one of these programs, program personnel will no doubt begin an educational evaluation to determine the everyday activities and teaching approach that are to be employed.

WHO IS SCREENING?

It is important for those who are most interested in treatment and education to be aware that many professional persons have been engaged in screening for a number of years. This is particularly true for children who are three and fewer years of age. Most commonly, such screening is performed by physicians and public health nurses. There are also a variety of state and local programs, as well as volunteer groups and researchers engaged in screening. The following list, which varies from community to community and state to state, is only a partial representation.

>State Health Department
>Social Rehabilitation Services with Early Periodic Screening
>Diagnosis and Treatment (EPSDT) Program
>Head Start
>Home Start
>Parent and Child Centers
>Hospitals (newborn nurseries)
>Easter Seal Society
>State Society for the Prevention of Blindness
>Volunteers for Vision
>Schools
>Speech and Hearing Centers

PULLING IT ALL TOGETHER

The teacher who seeks handicapped children for his early education project will have to consider how he can find the children who are best suited for his program. If the program is well established in the community, the procurement of children may not pose a problem. If, on the other hand, the program is new, the identification of children may present a major obstacle which must be overcome if the education program is to be successful. Initially, the educator may be inclined to establish his own screening program to find such children. That may, however, not be an easy task since parents may not be inclined to take their children to such a screening clinic. The difficulty with this approach is that the educator may find himself investing a major portion of his time and financial resources to carry out something that is a duplication of existing community screening efforts. In addition, if the child is to undergo a comprehensive evaluation by physicians, psychologists, audiologists, etc., the educator will still be forced to coordinate his activities with various professional personnel in the community. In the long run, it is generally most economical and efficient for the educator to establish an advisory board made up of a family practitioner, a pediatrician, a representative from the county and state health departments, a representative from EPSDT, and representatives from various specialties such as audiology, psychology, ophthalmology, etc., to develop a coordinated plan for ongoing screening, diagnosis, treatment, and education. Such advisory boards can then develop guidelines as to who screens whom, where, when, and how. In addition, they can coordinate the diagnostic follow-up and treatment with the educational program. Through such coordination of professional activities, the services and available funds can be utilized to the best advantage and the handicapped children will receive the greatest benefit.

APPENDIX A

Hearing Checklist from *A Guide to Screening EPSDT—Medicaid*
United States Department of Health Education and Welfare.

Questions for Parents of Infants

Six Months through Twenty-four Months

By four months does your baby:

1. Stir or awaken when he* is sleeping quietly and someone talks or makes a loud noise? (The baby doesn't always have to do this, but you should be able to notice it occasionally.)

2. Sometimes start or jump when there is a very loud sound, like a cough, a dog bark, or a dish falling to the floor?

By seven months does your baby:

1. Turn his head toward a sound or when his name is called when he cannot see you?

2. Stir or awaken when he is sleeping quietly and someone talks or makes a loud sound?

3. Sometimes start or jump when there is a very loud sound?

By nine months does your baby:

1. Directly find a sound made at his side, or turn his head when you call him from behind?

2. Stir or awaken when he is sleeping quietly and someone talks or makes a loud sound?

3. Sometimes jump or start when there is a very loud sound?

By twelve months does your baby:

---

*To avoid repetition of the awkward phrases "his or her," "him or her" and "he or she," we have used "his," "him" and "he."

1. Turn his head in any direction and find an interesting sound or the person speaking?

2. Begin to repeat some of the sounds you make?

3. Stir or awaken when he's sleeping quietly and someone talks or makes a loud sound?

By two years does your baby:

1. Point to at least one part of his body (eyes, feet, etc.) when you tell him to, without his seeing your lips?

2. Point to the right picture if you ask, "Where's the cat?" (or dog, or man, or horse) without his seeing your lips?

3. Give you a toy when you ask him to, or put a block on the table or chair when you ask him to, without his seeing your lips?

APPENDIX B

ADDITIONAL READING

1. Bailey, E. N., et al. Screening in pediatric practice. *Pediat. Clinics of N. Amer.,* 1974, 21, 123.

2. Frankenburg, W. K., and Camp. B. W. *Pediatric screening tests.* Springfield: Charles C. Thomas. In press.

3. Frankenburg, W. K., and North, A. F., Jr. *A guide to screening EPSDT - Medicaid.* Washington: United States Department of Health, Education and Welfare, 1974.

4. Wilson, J. M. G., and Jungner, G. *Principles and practice of screening for disease.* Public Health Papers 34, World Health Organization, 1968.

CHAPTER **3**

Infant Assessment and Developmental Handicaps

Rune J. Simeonsson

"When do we know what a child *knows?*" This intriguing question, which was asked by Sigel (1974) in the title of a recent article, seems particularly appropriate as we consider assessment of the handicapped infant. Often, efforts in infant assessment have been focused on the question, "When do we know what an infant *does?*" We are all aware of the difficulties which delayed and/or atypical development impose upon assessment in infancy. Those committed to early intervention, however, believe that handicapped infants can be validly assessed and that specific intervention will be reflected by increments in such assessments. Validating these beliefs has been complicated because (a) the relatively small population of handicapped infants has not yielded a large data base, (b) commonalities of infant development are confounded by large individual differences among handicapped infants, and (c) communication regarding assessment has been limited among programs serving infants. It thus seems important to consider the question "When do we know what an infant *knows?*" as we approach the problem of assessment and its role in intervention with handicapped infants.

  This chapter focuses on the assessment process, particularly as it

  RUNE J. SIMEONSSON is an Assistant Professor of Education at the University of North Carolina and Associate Director of the Research Training Program at the Frank Porter Graham Child Development Center. His major professional interests are development and learning in infancy, Piagetian theory and developmental disabilities, and children and hospitalization.

relates to the cognitive and behavioral characteristics of infants in need of prescription and intervention. From a practical as well as a philosophical standpoint, the term *assessment* rather than *diagnosis* is used. Diagnosis is generally defined as a process whereby particular characteristics, usually deficits, are analyzed and specified. Labeling of children often becomes an end in itself with diagnosis. Assessment, on the other hand, is a process for evaluating strengths as well as deficits, without the necessity of labeling, to provide a basis for intervention planning. Certainly, diagnosis has a proper place in the specification of sensory, neurological, and/or muscular problems within a handicapped child. The results of such diagnosis reveal factors which may influence intervention; they do not, however, provide a basis for prescribing methods or strategies for remediating the handicaps of individual children.

There are at least two purposes for assessing infant development: (1) to generate measures for program evaluation (see final chapter) and (2) to identify prescriptive strategies for individual infants within a program. This chapter approaches the problems in developmental assessment of handicapped infants by considering several approaches to assessment and by proposing a framework for prescriptive as well as evaluative assessment. Accomplishment of this objective will be facilitated by the use of a model of infant development proposed by Stedman (1965). The value of this model resides in its simplification and systematization of infant behavior and in the holistic perspective it provides. Furthermore, it provides a means of comparing existing approaches to infant assessment (See Figure 1). The components of the model are (a) *inputs,* consisting of physical or psychological stimuli, (b) mental or physiological *processes,* and (c) *outputs,* reflecting responses.

The range of populations served and of individual differences between handicapped infants from one program to another has resulted in a variety of assessment approaches. For the purposes of this review, the approaches will be examined in terms of their focus: (a) achievement, (b) function, or (c) competence. Prior to the review, it may be useful to identify each approach within Stedman's model to show its primary emphasis (see Figure 1). The focus of achievement assessment is primarily outputs; of functional assessment, the relationship between input and output; and of competency assessment, the process between input and output. In the following comparisons, each approach is defined, typical items or tasks are described, examples are given, and advantages and limitations are examined.

ACHIEVEMENT

The term *achievement* has been selected for those tests and scales which

FIGURE 1

INFANT BEHAVIOR MODEL

(STEDMAN, 1965)

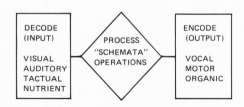

RELATIVE EMPHASES OF 3 ASSESSMENT APPROACHES

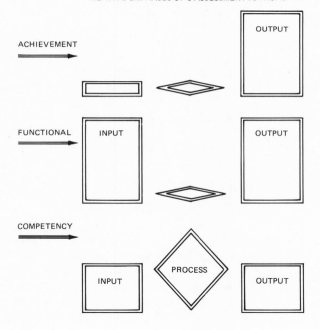

assess infant development on the basis of his passing or failing an achievement task. Such scales are typically downward extensions of the traditional
intelligence scales for older children and adults and have standardized
methods of administration and scoring. Assessment of the infant can be
done either by observation, report, or direct testing, and the focus is on
output, passing or failing. Assessment by this approach thus reflects the
level of an infant's achievement in terms of his normative age group, and
the summary score can be translated either into a developmental age or a

developmental quotient. The tests probably address the question of what an infant does relative to what others of his age do rather than what the infant knows independent of age considerations.

TYPICAL SCALES AND ITEMS

The Bayley Scales of Infant Development (Bayley, 1969) encompassing both mental and motor scales and situation codes, are probably the most widely used infant scales. Similar to earlier scales such as the Gesell (1952) and the Catell (1960), the Bayley covers the first thirty months of life, and achievement is defined in terms of age-specific levels.

The Griffith's Mental Developmental Scale (Griffiths, 1954) is a comprehensive instrument used with infants in Britain. The division of the test into five independently administered areas (locomotion, personal-social, hearing and speech, eye-hand, and performance), allows a profile of abilities to be prepared for each child. Selective administration of certain sub-scales to an infant with specific handicaps would seem possible.

The scoring procedure developed for the Denver Developmental Screening Test permits the derivation of mental age equivalents in personal-social, fine motor, language, gross motor, and overall development (Frankenburg, Camp, and VanNatta, 1971).

The Vineland Social Maturity Scale (Doll, 1956) relies on reported behavior for scoring and includes a substantial number of items in the infant and toddler range. Some major characteristics of these instruments are shown in Table 1.

Example: Scarr-Salapatek and Williams (1973) provided an interesting example of the use of this approach to assessment in an intervention study with low birth weight infants (<1800 g) who are at developmental risk. The experimental design involved the alternate assignment of thirty consecutively born infants to either a control group or to an experimental group, with the latter receiving specific sensory-motor stimulation during six weeks in a nursery plus weekly home visits during the first twelve months. Comparison of the two groups at the end of the year indicated that the stimulated group of infants had significantly higher developmental status, with an average difference of nearly ten Catell IQ points (mean values of 95.3 versus 85.7 for the stimulated and control groups, respectively). Further analysis indicated that, although the ranges of IQ scores were similar for both groups, only 22 percent of the stimulated infants had IQ values below 90, whereas 67 percent of the controls fell in this category.

Advantages: Advantages of achievement-based scales are that they are typically standardized, widely used, and have substantial communicability. Standardized tasks and administration reduce the subjectivity and allow

TABLE 1

CHARACTERISTICS OF SELECTED SCALES

SCALE	AGE RANGE (YRS)	NO. SUBSCALES	DEVELOPMENTAL INDEX
BAYLEY	0 - 2½	MENTAL, MOTOR	MDI, PDI
CATTELL	0 - 2½	–	IQ
GRIFFITHS	0 - 2	MOTOR, PERSONAL-SOCIAL, HEARING-SPEECH, EYE - HAND, PERF	GQ
DDST	0 - 6	LANGUAGE, PERSONAL-SOCIAL, FINE MOTOR, GROSS MOTOR	–
V.S.M.S.	0 - ADULT	–	SQ

for objective and quantified measurement. Derived scores, such as age equivalents, as well as IQ's or DQ's, are generally understood by workers in the field and therefore contribute to communicability of results. Some scales yield profiles for major areas of functioning.

Limitations: Several factors limit the appropriateness of achievement-based scales for assessment with handicapped infants. One factor is that the standardization procedure of some scales excluded handicapped and at-risk infants and thereby restricted generalizability of normative values. A second related factor is that normative tables do not include derived scores which are far below the normal range. A third factor is that the nature of the tasks and the standardized manner in which they are administered are often incompatable with the handicaps unique to certain infants;

thus the tests' utility is limited. A final limiting factor of achievement-oriented scales is that their pass/fail evaluation of tasks shows what the infant does, but this may not be a valid reflection of what he knows. For the infant whose development is substantially delayed or atypical, assessed achievement at a certain normative age level and failure to achieve it at another may be difficult to interpret, particularly in the context of varying rates of development and varying handicapping conditions. The result is often that individual differences are obscured rather than explained. At best, the indices which achievement scales yield present a broad picture of the child's general abilities, relative to those of normal peer groups.

FUNCTIONAL

A second approach which has seen increasing use is functional assessment. With this approach, an infant's behavior is systematically observed in the environmental context to determine the functional relationships which antecedent, contiguous, or consequential events have on his behavior. The focus of assessment is thus on the relationships between inputs and outputs (in terms of the components of the model proposed earlier). Associated with functional assessment is a technology of systematic observation. In addition to anecdotal or continuous recording, there are several more precise observation techniques (Hall, 1971). One is *frequency recording* in which a discrete event of a certain class (e.g., vocalization) is observed and counted, usually within a defined time period. Another technique is that of *duration recording* in which elapsed time rather than the frequency of a behavior is recorded. This method is perferred if the observed behavior is low in frequency but long in duration (e.g., visual fixation). A third technique is that of *interval recording* in which a specified observation session is divided into time units. Prescribed behavior categories are then checked as particular behaviors occur within each time interval; the occurence of these behaviors is summed for the total observation period. One example would be infant-object relationships in which the occurences of mouthing, handling, looking, banging, etc. are recorded. *Time sampling* is a variation of the interval recording technique. It allows random or scheduled observations over extended periods of time. Characteristics of these basic observation techniques and applications are summarized in Table 2.

   Example: A novel application of functional assessment has been reported with eight motorically handicapped subjects, aged 28-39 months (Jones, et al., 1969). Observations were made in an artifically designed "confined space" which was created by arranging portable walls to provide two-and-one-half square feet per occupant for eight children and one adult.

TABLE 2

OBSERVATION TECHNIQUES

TECHNIQUES	DEPENDENT VARIABLE	APPLICATION
CONTINUOUS RECORDING	VERBATIM ACCOUNT	ANECDOTAL RECORD
RATING	(1-5 SCALE) PREDETERMINED VALUES	TRAITS, EMOTIONS, ETC.
FREQUENCY	NUMBER COUNT	VOCALI- ZATIONS, STEPS, ETC.
DURATION	TIME: MINUTES, SECONDS	ON TASK; TANTRUM BEHAVIOR
INTERVAL	% OF TIME	MOTHER- INFANT INTER- ACTION
TIME SAMPLING	% OF TIME	GROUP PATTERNS

A rating code was prepared for the parameters of state of child, non-verbal and verbal communication, and social interaction, and they were recorded for each unit of observation for each child. Observations revealed marked individual differences over the course of repeated sessions and suggested the utility of this form of assessment to document social and communicative growth.

In another research study, functional assessment was made of the vocal behavior of six developmentally delayed infants, aged eleven to twenty-two months. (Wiegerink, et al., 1974). Analysis of the frequency and intervals of vocalization during two daily, ten-minute sessions over a period of twenty-eight days demonstrated the validity of this approach to infant assessment in reflecting differential infant response to novel or familiar (mother) reinforcing agents.

Advantages: There seem to be several advantages associated with functional assessment. First, there is a high level of face validity. Functional relationships between input and output can be operationally defined and cast into one of the techniques of observation. Functional assessment, in other words, can be tailored to the individual. Adaptations can be made to reflect the unique interactions of a handicapped infant with his social as well as his non-social environment. A final advantage is the applicability of functional assessment to empirical validation through the methodology of operant conditioning. Behavior of an infant is (1) observed during baseline to establish its rate, (2) differentially reinforced during period of intervention, and (3) reversed to reinstate original baseline conditions. Thus, the impact of intervention is demonstrated. Following reversal, the intervention is (4) again reinstated to generalize a behavior across situations and/or environments.

Limitations: It is often difficult to establish reliability of observation. The specification of behavior and the precision of timed observation require some training to obtain adequate reliability. This is particularly true in the context of complex interactional language and social behaviors. A second limitation is that functional assessment is often individual and situation-specific; thus, generalizability to other infants and other settings is limited. A third limitation is that this approach is not intrinsically developmental in nature; that is, assessment of a particular functional relationship does not examine preceding behavior nor does it predict subsequent behaviors in a hierarchical fashion.

COMPETENCY

The cognitive competency model, an outgrowth of Piagetian theory, is finding increased application as an assessment technique. With this approach, the process rather than the product of cognitive function is primarily assessed. These cognitive competencies can be qualitatively differentiated and shown to follow an invariant sequence in development. Transitions in this ordinal sequence from lower to higher stages are determined by the interaction of the infant with his environment. The rate of development of infants may, therefore, vary, but the sequence remains constant. The objective of competency-based assessment is, therefore, not to determine what strategy(ies) the infant uses in attempting to complete the task. The strategy provides the basis for determining the stage of cognitive functioning. The particular strategies an infant uses in imitative and intentional behavior, as well as those he uses dealing with space, time, object permanence and causality, are all examples of competencies which can be differentiated according to stage of development.

Representative Scales: The Infant Psychological Development Scale (IPDS) (Uzgiris and Hunt, 1966) and the Albert Einstein Scale of Sensory-Motor Intelligence (Corman and Escalona, 1969) are two instruments which can be used in assessing cognitive competency in ordinal sequence. The IPDS covers the age range of two weeks to two years and taps the following functional areas: object permanence, object means, imitation, causality, objects in space, and schemas (Wachs, 1973). The Albert Ein-

FIGURE 2

REPRESENTATIVE COMPETENCIES MEASURED BY
ALBERT-EINSTEIN SCALE AT VARIOUS
SENSORY-MOTOR STAGES.

Stage		PREHENSION	SPACE	OBJECT PERMANENCE	
INVENTION OF NEW MEANS THROUGH MENTAL COMBINATIONS			SOLVES DE-TOUR PRO-BLEM TO RETRIEVE OBJECT	CORRECTLY RECOVERS OBJECT CHILD NOT IN SIGHT WHEN OBJECT HIDDEN	VI
			INVISIBLE-DISPLACEMENT		
TERTIARY CIRCULAR REACTIONS			FOLLOWS TRAJECTORY OF OBJECT AROUND DETOUR TO RETRIEVE IT	CORRECTLY RECOVERS OBJECT PLACED UNDER 1 OF 3 SCREENS	V
			VISIBLE DISPLACEMENT		
COORDINATION OF SECONDARY SCHEMATA			RE-ESTABLISHES HAND CONTACT WHEN OBJECT IS PLACED IN DIFFERENT SPATIAL ARRANGEMENTS	RECOVERS OBJECT HIDDEN UNDER SINGLE SCREEN	IV
SECONDARY CIRCULAR REACTIONS		TRANSFERS OBJECT WITH VISUAL REGARD	TURNS TO LOCATE OBJECT PLACED BESIDE HIM	FOLLOWS TRAJECTORY OF DROPPED OBJECT	III
PRIMARY CIRCULAR REACTION		HELD OBJECT BROUGHT TO MOUTH			II
USE OF REFLEXES					I

stein Scale covers a similar age range through the three separate scales of prehension, object permanence, and spatial relationships. Both scales assess competency at the highest level of attainment. This ordinal approach to infant assessment can perhaps be clarified by examining a matrix of Piaget's sensory-motor stages and the functions assessed through the use of the Albert Einstein Scale. See Figures 2 and 3. A more elaborate model of this matrix is available in Phillip's (1969) summary of Piaget's theory.

Example: An interesting illustration of the applicability of this approach to work with handicapped infants in found in the validation study reported on by Corman and Escalona (1969). In longitudinal testing, involving eye-hand coordination, of fourteen infants on the prehension scale, the age of entry into each new stage was documented for each infant. One of these infants was found to be significantly retarded in development, and it was evident that his age of entry into sequential stages was markedly delayed in comparison to the group means. Examination of Table 3 reveals the invariant sequence in the acquisition of these competencies. The ranges

FIGURE 3

PREHENSION SCALE:
AGE IN MONTHS AT ENTRY INTO EACH NEW STAGE

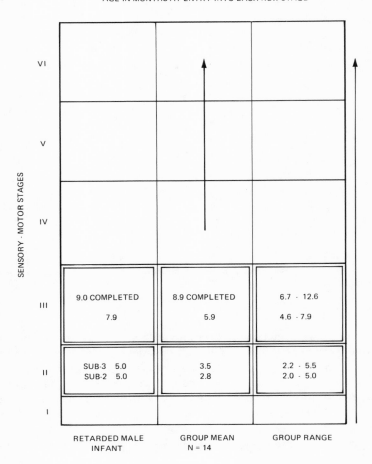

ASSESSMENT APPROACH	DEVELOPMENTAL PROGRESSION	VARIOUS DISABILITIES	TIME REQUIREMENT	INDIVIDUAL DIFFERENCES	NON-SPECIALIST ADMINISTRATION	DIRECT PROGRAMMING IMPLICATIONS	SENSITIVE TO SHORT TERM CHANGES	ACCEPTABILITY AS EVALUATION INDEX
ACHIEVEMENT	+	+	+	-	+	-	-	+
FUNTIONAL	-	+	+	+	+	+	+	0
COMPETENCY	+	+	-	+	0	+	+	0

MEETS CRITERIA
+ POSITIVE
- NEGATIVE
0 UNDETERMINED

TABLE 3

COMPARISONS OF INFANT ASSESSMENT
APPROACHES WITH SELECTED CRITERIA.

show that individual differences in rate varied substantially.

Advantages: A major advantage of this approach is the focus on the individual infant. This advantage is of particular value in the assessment of the handicapped infant whose unique disabilities interact with the environment to confound the emergence of "functions" which may appear at different rates within a given child. This approach permits the profiling of cognitive patterns as suggested by Wachs (1973). Furthermore, the sequential developmental progression upon which the approach is based provides a firm basis for identifying competencies achieved and those yet to be acquired.

Limitations: Availability of these instruments for wide use has been limited. Acceptability of the instruments for program documentation to funding agencies has not been established. This approach requires familiarity with and commitment to a theoretical perspective. The actual administration is also demanding in time as well as in effort because optimal rather than elicited performance, as with a standarized test task, is being assessed.

REVIEW OF APPROACHES

It seems worthwhile to compare these approaches in their ability to deal with the question "When do we know what an infant knows?" To make the comparisons meaningful, each approach is rated according to the following criteria: (a) shows developmental progression, (b) can be used with various disabilities, (c) has a time requirement, (d) reflects individual differences, (e) can be administered by a non-specialist, (f) has direct programming implications, (g) is sensitive to short-term changes, (h) is currently acceptable as an index for accountability. From this somewhat arbitrary comparison (Table 3), it seems evident that functional and competency-based approaches provide the most positive directions for assessment in infant intervention programs. With this conclusion in mind, we will proceed to some practical considerations in designing a framework of assessment.

A FRAMEWORK FOR ASSESSMENT

We have highlighted differences between three approaches in this review, perhaps to an artificial degree. It is obvious that, in many instances, the tasks administered as well as the responses obtained are highly similar across approaches. Differences reside in the information collected, the inferences made about the information, and the use made of the information in intervention. The functional and the competency-based approaches have a common focus: i.e., the existing behaviors and competencies in the child which are relatively independent of the child's age, diagnosis, or handicap. Standardized "achievement" scales, on the other hand, use age and handicap variables in generating a deficit index. They are thus more likely to encourage labeling or deficits which may contribute negatively to intervention through a self-fulfilling prophecy.

The value of the Piagetian-based competency approach as a framework for assessment is enhanced by the humanitarian impact of the normalization principle (Kugel and Wolfensberger, 1969) in intervention with the handicapped. The normalizaton principle and Piagetian theory, although different in many respects, share a common focus on the competencies of the individual and on the individual's transition from dependency to independence. These two influences may contribute to an expanded framework for assessment of development. Some steps in this framework are (1) consideration of pertinent variables, (2) problems of assessing special populations, and (3) practical suggestions.

PERTINENT VARIABLES

(A) State: A methodological issue usually restricted to research with newborns and very young infants is that of "state," a variable essentially equivalent to level of consciousness. The states are regular sleep, irregular sleep, drowsiness, alert inactivity, waking activity, and crying; each of

these meet distinct behavioral criteria. Changes in state often confound newborn research in that the response or the activity of the infant is shown to be a function of his state when he is tested (Korner, 1972). With the handicapped infant, state may continue to play an important confounding role in the assessment of functional status well beyond the newborn period. This may be particularly true when an infant's state or level of consciousness has been permanently altered by neurological damage or when medication produces artificial variations in the state of the infant. Korner stresses the importance of observing infants in comparable states or of controlling for a state as is done when newborns are tested with the Neonatal Behavioral Assessment Scale (Brazelton, 1973). State may thus be a variable that can be used in validating the interpretation of other assessment data as well as providing a source of information which, in its own right, reflects development in handicapped infants.

(B) Contextualization: In a discussion of tests and assessment, Sigel (1974) proposed the following principle: "The context in which the item is presented alters the very nature of that item by virtue of necessitated situational constraints or facilitators" (Sigel, 1974, p. 206). Stated more simply, the context in which we assess the child may determine the response obtained. Sigel provides an illustration which is probably familiar to many of us. Two-year-olds involved in an early childhood project generally failed the *concept of one* on the Bayley Scale. This was a surprise to teachers who recalled that in the context of the classroom, some children knew the *concept of one* as well as two in relating to such things as cookies, etc. Similar discrepancies were obtained in visual memory tasks as well as in language tasks, all of which led Sigel to pose the question, "When do we know what the child knows?"

(C) Time: In functional as well as competency-based assessment, time can be used as an index of progress, whether it involves the acquisition of a reinforced behavior or a specified competence or the time elapsed for transition from one sensory-motor stage to the next. In the past, infant progress was measured by changes in behavior after a period of intervention. A reversed focus would be measurement of the amount of time to acquire or change a particular behavior. Such shifting of independent and dependent variables permits a different perspective on assessing intervention and has implications for identifying and predicting performance with handicapped populations (Simeonsson and Cromwell, in press).

PROBLEM OF SPECIAL POPULATIONS

The second issue considered in the framework for assessment is the problem of special populations. One group of handicapped infants presenting particular problems are those with cerebral palsy and other neuromuscular disorders. The problems of involuntary movement, spasticity, and prosthetics, as well as the lack of appropriate measures of motor development, have made it extremely difficult to assess validly the abilities of such handicapped infants and to measure changes following intervention. Two recent studies have described methods, which could be incorporated into intervention programs, to quantify developmental assessment in children with cerebral palsy. Reimers (1972) devised a scoring system to evaluate the results of orthopedic treatments in cerebral palsy. Scoring was based on the amount of support needed to walk, sit, and stand, with higher scores reflecting much support and lower scores reflecting less support and approaching normality. A more detailed and methodologically sophisticated evaluation method for young infants was reported by Wright and Nicholson (1973). Four- to seven-point scales were devised for a variety of motor functions (head control, crawling, range of movement, etc.) to provide assessments over time.

A related issue is the postural limitations often existing in physically handicapped youngsters. The nature and degree of handicap may often restrict the response or activity in certain positions or postures which the infant otherwise would attempt to make. It would thus be important to manipulate and/or control position and posture systematically to sort out volitional, as opposed to motoric, limitations. This problem is analogous to that of state, referred to earlier, and should be documented.

Other problem populations are severely disturbed or battered infants. Although it is not the intent here to explore the etiology or the diagnosis of battering, it is clear that emotionally disturbed and battered infants present emotional as well as cognitive needs (Martin, 1972). The Infant Behavior Survey developed by Carey (1970) is one approach to assessment of temperament, and Thomas et al. (1963) provide a framework for assessing mood, activity, intensity, distractability, etc. The Infant Behavior Record developed by Bayley (1969) also provides a valuable adjunct to assessment of social behavior and cognitive style in the infant.

Another population which may emerge as "at risk" for developmental intervention is the infant facing foster or adoptive placement. Legal maneuverings and agency protocol may often result in multiple mothering, inconsistent stimulation, and delay or disruption of the attachment process at a time when consistency of stimulation and caretaking are very important. Such factors are likely to contribute to significant delays in cognitive, social, and affective development.

PRACTICAL SUGGESTIONS

(1) Specify the purpose of assessment. If it is for the generation of inter-

vention strategies, competency assessment may be valuable. If the purpose is program evaluation, standardized scales may be suitable. Be parsimonious; use only the approaches that serve your purpose. (2) Translate results of assessment into methods and evaluative criteria which can be used in monitoring the progress of an infant's intervention. (3) Specify the time period in which competencies are to be achieved. Progress can then be assessed in relation to predicted gains. [In another context, we have proposed models for assessment and monitoring of development which use a systems model with actual and expected gain comparisons (Simeonsson and Wiegerink, 1975).] (4) Involve parents in the assessment process, not only as respondents but as active observers and evaluators of infant progress. (5) Be willing to experiment. There is no monopoly on assessment instruments or techniques. Adapt, modify, or create instruments which validly reflect the unique assessment needs of your population. Such instruments, however, should have demonstrated validity and should be communicable. (6) Think ordinally and avoid the expectation of equal increments of developmental growth over time. Ordinal development from one stage to the next may be rapid at certain times and very slow at others. Ongoing assessment, with time as a variable, may be best suited for making these measures. (7) Assess the variability of an infant's functioning across competencies as well as across time. A single index or mean performance may not reflect changes in terms of a period of intervention. Other indices, such as the mental age range on a scale between first failure and highest success, may reflect substantial reduction from one assessment to the next without significant single index change. Thus, an assessment which notes the disappearance of an immature response may be just as important as one which shows the acquisition of a more mature response. This kind of assessment is particularly important for motor handicapped infants. Similarly, assessment in which a profile is generated is more likely to reflect changes as a function of intervention than is a single index.

SUMMARY

This paper presented three basic approaches to assessment of development in infancy. Each approach was examined within a model stressing input, process, and output of an infant's development. It was suggested that an achievement-based approach taps primarily output phases, whereas a functional approach assesses the relationship between input and output. Competency-based assessment was proposed as the most appropriate approach to assessment of handicapped infants because it does not label or provide a deficit perspective. Instead, it identifies existing competencies, and its ordinality provides a context for intervention programming. In a suggested framework for assessment, state and contextualization were stressed as variables to control and measure relative to assessment. The use of time as a dependent rather than an independent variable was recommended. The special problems of physically handicapped and emotionally stressed infants were examined within the context of assessment. Practical suggestions indicated that assessment should be closely aligned to and reflective of purposive, objective, and predictive concerns for the individual infant. Thus, we may come to Piaget's (1972) reflection on the problem of knowledge and the development of intelligence. "It reduces to analyzing *how* the subject becomes progressively able to *know* objects adequately, that is how he becomes capable of objectivity." (p. 704). This summarizes a desirable objective for assessment and intervention in infancy.

BIBLIOGRAPHY

Bayley, N. *Bayley scales of infant development: Manual.* New York: The Psychological Corporation, 1969.

Brazelton, T. B. *Neonatal behavioral assessment scale.* Clinics in Developmental Medicine, No. 50. Philadelphia. J. B. Lippincott, Co., 1973.

Carey, W. B. A simplified method for measuring infant temperament. *Journal of Pediatrics,* 1970, 77 (2), pp. 188-194.

Cattell, P. *The measurement of intelligence of infants and young children.* Revised 1960. New York: Johnston Reprint Corporation. 1970.

Corman, H. H., and Escalona, S. K. Stages of sensory-motor development: A replication study. *Merrill-Palmer Quarterly of Behavior and Development,* 1969, 15, 351-361.

Doll, E. A. *The measurement of social competence: A manual for the Vineland Social Maturity Scale.* Minneapolis: Educational Test Bureau, Educational Publishers, Inc., 1953.

Frankenburg, W. K., Camp, B. W., and VanNatta, P. A. Validity of the Denver Developmental Screening Test. *Child Development,* 1971, 42, 475-485.

Gesell, A., and Amatruda, C. S. *Developmental diagnosis.* London: Cassell and Company, Ltd., 1952.

Griffiths, R. *The abilities of babies.* London: University of London Press, 1954.

Hall, R. V. *Managing behavior I:Behavior modification: The measurement of behavior.* Lorens, Kansas: H & H Enterprises, 1971.

Jones, N. H., Barrett, N. L., Olonoff, C., and Andersen, E. Two experiments in training handicapped children at nursery school. In P. Wolff, & R. MacKeith, (Eds.), *Planning for better learning,* (Clinics in Developmental Medicine, No. 33). London: William Heinemann Medical Books, Ltd., 1969.

Korner, A. F. State as variable, as obstacle, and a mediator of stimulation in infant research. *Merrill-Palmer Quarterly of Behavior and Development.* 1972, 18 (2), 77-94.

Kugel, R., and Wolfensberger, W. (Eds.). *Changing patterns in residential services for the mentally retarded.* Washington, D. C.: United States Printing Office, 1969.

Martin, H. The child and his development. In C. H. Kempe, & R. E. Helfer, (Eds.), *Helping the battered child and his family.* Philadelphia. J. B. Lippincott Co., 1972, 93-114.

Phillips, J. L., Jr. *The origins of intellect: Piaget's theory.* San Francisco: W. H. Freeman & Company, 1969.

Piaget, J. Piaget's theory. In P. H. Mussen, (Ed.), *Carmichael's manual of child psychology.* New York: John Wiley & Sons, Inc., 1970.

Reimers, J. A scoring system for the evaluation of ambulation in cerebral palsied patients. *Developmental Medicine and Child Neurology,* 1972, 14, 332-335.

Scarr-Salapatek, S., and Williams, M. L. The effects of early stimulation on low-birth-weight infants. *Child Development,* 1973, 44, 94-101.

Sigel, I. E. When do we know what a child knows? *Human Development,*

44

1974, 17, 201-217.

Simeonsson, R. J., and Wiegerink, R. Accountability: A dilemma in infant intervention. *Exceptional Children.* In press.

Simeonsson, R. J., and Cromwell, R. L. Developmental factors — Cognition and intelligence. In B. B. Wolman, (Ed.). *International encyclopedia of neurology, psychiatry, psychoanalysis & psychology.* In press.

Stedman, D. J. *An approach to the study of infant behavior.* Durham N. C.: The Education Improvement Program, 1965.

Thomas, A., Chess, S., Birch, H. G., Hertzig, N. E., and Korn, S. *Behavioral individuality in early childhood.* New York: New York University Press, 1963.

Uzgiris, I., and Hunt, J. McV. An instrument for assessing infant psychological development. Mimeographed paper. University of Illinois, 1966.

Wachs, T. D. The measurement of early intellectual functioning: Contributions from developmental psychology. In G. Tarjan, E. K. Eyman, & C. E. Meyers, (Eds.), *Socio-behavioral studies in mental retardation.* Washington: Monographs of the American Association on Mental Deficiency, No. 1, 1973, 28-45.

Wiegerink, R., Harris, C., Simeonsson, R., and Pearson, M. E. Social stimulation of vocalizations in delayed infants: Familiar and novel agent. *Child Development,* 1974, 45, 866-872.

Wright, T., and Nicholson, J. Physiotherapy for the spastic child: An evaluation. *Developmental Medicine and Child Neurology,* 1973, 15, 146-153.

CHAPTER 4

The Infant Stimulation/Mother Training Project

Earladeen Badger

PROGRAM HISTORY AND DESCRIPTION OF PRESENT PROGRAM

During the latter part of 1972, the Cincinnati Maternal and Infant Care Project brought together a multi-disciplinary team of professionals interested in initiating a comprehensive intervention program for high-risk, adolescent mothers and their infants. Participating agencies were Cincinnati General Hospital (CGH), Cincinnati Health Department, Fels Research Institute, Children's Hospital Research Foundation, and the Newborn Division at the Department of Pediatrics in the University of Cincinnati College of Medicine. The research project established by this group was service-oriented and preventive in nature. It incorporated an infant stimulation curriculum and mothers' training model which had been developed and tested at the University of Illinois and at parent and child centers in Illinois and Georgia. Intervention began at birth and emphasized medical and nutritional services as well as improved family style through mother competence.

The forty-eight mother-infant pairs for this study were recruited at

EARLADEEN BADGER is an Instructor at the University of Cincinnati College of Medicine, Department of Pediatrics (Newborn Division), and she is also Coordinator of the Infant Stimulation/Mother Training Project in Cincinnati. Her major professional interests lie in three organizations: United Services for Effective Parenting (Cincinnati); the National Alliance Concerned with School Age Children (state and regional); and the Consortium on Early Childbearing and Childrearing (national).

TABLE I

EXPERIMENTAL DESIGN INCLUDES A TOTAL OF FORTY-EIGHT SOCIALLY DISADVANTAGED MOTHER-INFANT PAIRS RECRUITED DURING THE LYING-IN PERIOD AND RANDOMLY ASSIGNED TO EITHER CLASS OR HOME VISITING TREATMENT GROUPS.

TREATMENT GROUPS

SUBJECT GROUPS	CLASSES	VISITS
	MOTHER TRAINING PROGRAM, WEEKLY CLASSES	MONTHLY SUPPORT-IVE HOME VISITS
OLD MOTHERS: 18 YEARS OR OLDER, MATURE INFANTS	12 MOTHERS AND INFANTS	12
YOUNG MOTHERS: 16 YEARS OR YOUNGER, MA-TURE INFANTS	12	12

the postpartum unit of CGH during January and February 1973 (Table 1). Twenty-four mother-infant pairs were to attend weekly classes and twenty-four were to serve as a home-visited comparison group. Almost every mother who met the selection criteria agreed to participate, and thus a random sample of the delivery population was assured. Infants were first-born, gestationally mature, and had five-minute Apgars scores over seven. Groups were matched for race and sex with nine blacks and three Appalachian whites in each of the four groups. All were socially disadvantaged in terms of social class status.

Weekly classes for the twenty-four mother-infant pairs assigned to the educational intervention program began February 1, 1973 and continued until the infants were eighteen months of age. Young (sixteen years and under) and old (eighteen years and over) mothers and their infants met separately. Classes were arranged to coincide with evening pediatric clinics at CGH so that doctors, nurses, and social workers were available for consultation. *The major intent of these sessions was to stimulate the development of infants by supporting and extending the mothers' role as primary teacher.*

The comparison group received the services of an interested resource person—a nurse or social worker. During monthly home visits, infant development was assessed, and problems related to health and nutrition were discussed, but no instruction in the implementation of the infant stimulation curriculum was offered to these mothers. The infants did, however, receive toys like those provided to the other group. Favorable responses from the mothers who participated in the home-visited group were received regularly, and we are convinced that the service aspect of home visits has had a positive influence on infant performance.

Testing data taken when infants were twelve months old suggested that infants of adolescent mothers (sixteen years and younger) began to fall behind very early in life and were indeed "in jeopardy." This was not, however, the case for infants of young mothers who attended classes. Accordingly, in September 1974, the pilot program was incorporated into a service model which includes all adolescent mothers (sixteen and younger) who deliver at CGH and who live within a three-mile radius of the hospital. The high rate of delivery within this age group ensures a new class of twelve mother-infant pairs each month. These groups are offered a minimum series of eight "parenting" classes. As in the pilot study, mothers are recruited during the lying-in period, and classes begin when infants are three-four weeks old. Mothers bring their infants with them to classes which meet within the facilities provided by CGH's evening pediatric clinic. A doctor, nurse, and social worker are available for individual consultation when the need for it is indicated, and trained volunteers complement professional group leaders to maintain an intensive level of programming.

GOALS AND OBJECTIVES

Since the feasibility of initiating intervention during the first year of life had not been clearly demonstrated, the original study was undertaken to determine whether an intensive, broadly defined educational program for adolescent mothers and their infants could be successful within the pediatric setting of a large medical center. A previously validated educational curriculum for infants and a mother training model served as vehicles for introducing a broad health-education program, since we acknowledged the mutually reinforcing nature of health, nutrition, and educational intervention, as well as the importance of early maternal-infant attachment, in maximizing the potential of high-risk infants. Furthermore, intervention for the class groups of mother-infant pairs was structured (1) to provide multiple opportunities for young women to experience satisfactions in their new role as mothers, (2) to train mothers to foster the sensorimotor, cognitive, and language development of their infants through an educational curriculum which matches developmental levels with sequenced skills, (3) to develop the mother's sense of dignity and self-esteem in their primary roles as teachers of their infants, (4) to provide a setting where personal and family problems beyond the mother-infant focus could be openly discussed and resolved, (5) to increase the mothers' awareness of the health, nutritional, psychological, and educational needs of their infants, and (6) to replace crisis-oriented medical treatment with comprehensive health care.

TEACHING-LEARNING FORMAT

The expanded service model follows the same general format as the pilot study except that the postnatal classes offered to all adolescent mothers (sixteen years and younger) and their infants delivered at CGH run for an abbreviated period—from eight-twenty weeks.

Classes meet in one of the two waiting rooms available for pediatric clinic patients at CGH and are scheduled from 7-8:30 p.m. to avoid conflicts with the schedules of young mothers who often return to school or secure part-time employment during the day. In a given class of twelve mother-infant pairs, mean attendance is 8.6, and cab pools help to ensure this rate. Visitors are encouraged to attend and may include the girl- and boyfriends of the mothers or the fathers of the infants.

Program commitment is ensured in a number of ways.

1. Babies are photographed regularly by the instructor, and mothers receive copies of their favorite prints.

2. Program toys and materials are given to the mothers to use with their infants at home.

3. Two booklets, *Mother's Guide to Early Learning* and *Development of Language,* are given to each mother as supplements to class viewing of selected infant care films and slide series.

4. Mothers earn high school credit in child development for every thirty hours of class participation.

5. Individual attention by the clinic doctor or pediatric nurse is available to any infant at his mother's request.

6. Involvement in group instruction is essentially non-threatening

and provides ongoing opportunities for attitudinal change and personal growth.

In the mothers' training model, mothers are led to understand that how they interact with their infants now will make an important difference in later life; they are encouraged to respond to their infants' vocalizing as well as to the babies' behavioral indicators of interest and stress as they interact with play materials. Finally, they are taught a sequence of infant development skills which enables them to choose appropriate materials for stimulating their child's development.

There are teaching strategies and techniques which characterize the role the instructor plays in the mothers' training model. As group leader, she is both a resource person and a mother model. Using an informal rather than a didactic approach, she teaches through *demonstration.* For example, a baby begins to vocalize. The instructor responds by establishing face to face contact with the infant at a distance of approximately eight to ten inches and repeats the infant's vocal pattern. As pseudo-imitative behavior occurs alternately between instructor and infant, the mother is encouraged to become involved. She is asked to replace the instructor in *repetition* of the demonstration. As she tries, the instructor uses positive *reinforcement* to encourage and extend her best efforts. In the event that an individual mother appears indifferent or fails to respond appropriately to the attentional needs of her infant, the instructor may call on other mothers for help. *Group pressure* or acceptance by one's peers is a powerful motivator in altering an adolescent mother's behavior towards her infant. On occasion, the instructor may use *confrontation* to change an individual mother's inappropriate behavior towards her infant. For example, an infant begins to fuss. The mother responds by combing the baby's hair. He cries louder and she continues combing. The instructor might intervene by stating firmly, "You don't provoke a fussing baby further by combing his hair. He wants to be cuddled when he's unhappy."

The teaching techniques used by the instructor are soon incorporated into the repertoire of some of the mothers in the group. This incorporation may occur as early as the second or third class. Mothers who are particularly adept as infant stimulators are easily identified, and their actions are observed and imitated by the other mothers. Further, individual mothers demonstrate stimulation activities with one another's infants. Comaraderie with their peers helps adolescent mothers reinforce each other in play behavior with their children. And, when mutual respect exists, they can openly confront or censure a mother who appears to be ignoring or behaving inappropriately toward her infant.

Our experience thus far has focused on infants who are gestationally

50

mature at birth. These infants are physically robust and typically develop well with the supportive health care and nutritional services offered by Cincinnati's Maternal and Infant Care Project. Our infant stimulation efforts, then, are primarily directed towards sensorimotor, language, psycho-social, and cognitive development and, in general, follow the developmental sequence summarized thus:

From Three or Four Weeks to Three Months. Mothers bring their babies to class in infant seats. If a mother does not have an infant seat, the project supplies one and she is free to take it home on loan. Mothers are told that using an infant seat during the first three months promotes the child's social development, for he becomes more aware of what is going on outside the crib.

A large conference table in the classroom becomes a place where mothers can position babies in their infant seats and face them as they sit around the table. Face to face contact is facilitated, baby can nap comfortably if he's sleepy, and mother is close enough to respond to his attentional needs.

During these first months, mothers are alerted to the individual differences in infants and to the importance of responding promptly and appropriately to the needs of their infants. They are told that maternal-infant attachment occurs as they accept and derive satisfaction from their role as the primary caretaker of their infants. In turn, baby learns that mother can be trusted to answer his needs, an awareness which helps him to develop greater confidence in mastering his environment independently later on.

Mothers learn that their infants' reflexive behavior is incorporated in and adapted to learned social and manipulative skills. Their interactions can stimulate the development of early sensorimotor skills as follows:

1.   Offering sucking devices other than the bottle or pacifier will increase the infant's interest in varied mouthing experiences. A small piece of dampened sponge, an old fashioned wooden clothespin, and a small plastic rattle are given to each mother. Since baby is reflexively equipped to grasp at least momentarily, he will soon bring any of these objects to his mouth if his mother places it in his fist.

2.   The newborn infant is alert to the voice of his mother and begins to study her face as she talks to him. His cries soon become cooing sounds as she soothes him. As he attends and watches her mouth move, he begins to make vowel sounds. Mothers are encouraged to engage in vocal play with their infants. Recognizing that a happy infant is a well-stimulated infant, mothers make high-contrast visual-stimulation pictures which they attach to the side panels of the cribs. They also attach a cotton cord across the width of the cribs and attach interesting visual objects—ballons,

swatches of material, plastic streamers—with plastic clothes pins. Rubber squeaky toys and plastic rattle dolls are given to the mothers as interesting objects to attract their infants' attention and to promote visual following behavior when they are rotated in a 180 degree arc at a distance of ten-twelve inches from the infants.

3. As a preface to visually-directed reaching and the grasping of objects near the midline of the body, infants begin to notice and study their hands. To encourage this behavior, each mother is given small bells to attach to elastic bands and place on her baby's wrists. Babies wave their arms more in order to produce the tinkling sound of the bells. In the process, eyes connect with hands. About this time, mothers are given long-handled rattles to offer their babies. If mother touches baby's hand with the rattle as she offers it, he will find it easier to open his fist and grasp the rattle. Coincidental with the infant's earliest success in purposeful grasping of an object comes his purposeful shaking of a rattle. In terms of cause and effect behavior or cognitive development, he has come to understand that if he shakes the rattle, he can produce sounds.

From Three to Six Months. The physical arrangement of the classroom changes when the infants are about three months of age. The conference table is replaced by an indoor-outdoor carpet (twelve inches diameter) encircled by a portayard. Chairs are arranged in a circle around the porta-yard. Teaching props during this period of infant development include: cotton rug yarn (stretched across the play area and attached to the porta-yard) from which visually stimulating materials and objects which encourage manipulation are suspended (crib activators, plastic streamers, swatches of material); large stuffed animals and foam rubber bolsters which support infants in a prone position so that their hands are off the floor and free for manipulative activity; one-and-one-half feet high unbreakable mirrors (like those used in shoe stores) positioned so that infants can view themselves and their activity; a variety of visually stimulating, action-response materials which invite manipulative and exploratory mouthing behavior.

During this period of development, mothers learn that babies want new and novel experiences and seem to thrive and develop in relation to the variety of sensory input they receive. Something to look at becomes something to touch. Something to hold becomes something to mouth. Something which produces sound becomes something to shake or bang. Mothers receive a variety of inexpensive materials for use in the home during this period: crib activator, rubber teether, suction toy, stuffed gingerbread doll, roly-poly toy, plastic tub toys. They are encouraged to adapt household items as instruments of activity for babies: e.g., making bottle babies for baby to look at by drawing faces with wax crayons on clean, empty plastic bottles; giving aluminum foil pie plates to baby for banging; offering measuring spoons, wooden spools, or large, clean plastic curlers for baby to mouth.

The mother-infant interaction which occurs typically in the twelve foot circular play area is facilitated by the arrangement of materials and props in the ring and by the positions assumed by mothers and infants. Mothers are free to get in or out of the play area during the one-and-one-half hour period. When a mother is out of the ring, she sits on one of the chairs surrounding the portayard; she might be watching other mothers and infants interact or she might be holding a baby who has fallen asleep. However, when she is in the ring, she sits on the rug and interacts with her own or another mother's baby in one of the following ways:

1. An assembly line stimulation routine is provided for those infants who appear less active and somewhat disinterested in the environment. Positioned in infant seats, they are moved, according to their interest or boredom, down the line of stimulating materials which are suspended from the cotton cord attached to the sides of the portayard. Mothers interact by smiling and hitting or shaking the suspended objects. Crib activators, bells, etc. are close enough to baby's reach so that he can accidentally fist-swipe at them to produce sounds. Mothers are instructed to provide verbal encouragement in order to arouse and maintain the infants' emotional and physical states.

2. Large stuffed animals and vinyl-covered, half-circle, rubber bolsters serve as body supports so that the infant can use his hands to reach for and manipulate objects while he is in a prone position. Lying flat on his tummy and unable to creep, baby soon becomes frustrated and begins to fuss, but an abdominal support elevates his head and torso and extends his arms in front of him so that he can busy his hands in exploring materials nearby. Mothers are encouraged to place action-response toys (floating balls, roly-poly toys) just out of reach so that baby will set them in motion with the still uncoordinated movements of his arms and hands. Visual and auditory stimulation from above, i.e., mother's face and voice or a squeaking rubber toy, cause further excitement and efforts at muscular control in this position.

3. Infants who are beginning to sit without support can practice manipulative skills if mothers further stabilize their balance by placing them between their legs (baby's back to mother's front). In such a position, baby's hands are free to work cooperatively in handling materials. He can mouth a plastic flower with one hand and bang an aluminum plate with the other, or he can begin to transfer a wooden bell block from one hand to the other, in early-examining fashion. When he is able to sit independently for fifteen-twenty minutes without tiring—at approximately five-

six months of age—mother changes her sitting position so she is facing him. In this position, she is better able to interact verbally and to encourage his efforts in mastering new manipulative skills, such as those offered in a Busy Box.

From Six to Twelve Months. The physical arrangement of the classroom continues to include the carpet encircled by the portayard with chairs for adults around the ring. The increased activity of the infants with their ability to maneuver about on all fours calls for an ever-changing array of materials which stimulate the development of (1) examining behavior, (2) fine manipulation coordination, (3) tactile awareness, (4) release of objects in relation to a target, (5) socialization, and (6) imitative learning.

During this period of development, mothers learn that their infants' interests in learning, persistence at tasks, and attention spans increase when the infants are free to manipulate a variety of objects in their environment and when they are encouraged to imitate models of behavior. The following materials are given to mothers for use at home in order to reinforce and extend learning experiences offered in class: a rattle ball and a small wheeled toy for imitative learning, bell blocks and one inch stacking blocks for fine manipulative coordination, a plastic toy telephone for socialization and imitation, plastic bottle and clothespins for release of objects in relation to a target, and a box of miscellaneous materials for examining behavior and tactile awareness. Further, mothers are encouraged to provide babies with the freedom of the floor, after making sure that safety rules are adhered to.

Infant-infant interaction is as much a part of the teaching-learning format in classes at this developmental level as is mother-infant interaction. Consider, for example, the following sequence of typical activities:

1. As mothers and infants arrive, babies are placed in the ring and mothers occupy seats around the portayard. The instructor and one mother volunteer are inside the ring with infants. They serve primarily as monitors and occasionally as re-directors of baby activity.

2. Infants begin to activate materials independently. They may crawl, sit, or walk. If they are primarily action-bound, they may be pushing a rattle ball, throwing and fetching a foam rubber ball, or just carrying materials around the circle. Less active infants may be sitting, manipulating and examining objects, or observing the activity around them. One infant may be oblivious to another infant sitting next to him, as in parallel play; however, social interaction is more often the case. Babies watch, smile at, babble with, and kiss one another. They also share materials (sometimes not so cooperatively) and pull one another's hair. On occasion, they will imitate an interesting behavior observed in another; e.g., banging a drum.

3. Mother-infant interaction occurs (a) when an infant fusses and needs and wants only mother's attention and (b) when mother is involved in a teaching activity; e.g., object permanence or hide and seek games, the facial and gestural actions involved in nursery rhymes, and the encouragement of imitative behavior. All maternal-infant interactions are determined by the infant's attentional needs and interests.

From Twelve to Eighteen Months. While use of the portayard set-up in the classroom continues, three child-size table and chair sets are added. Action-response toys (music boxes, toys, pop-up animals), balls, small wooden and friction cars, and seriated wooden boxes are examples of materials used in the ring. Form fitting boxes, art materials, books, pop and stringing beads, peg fitting sets, and plastic stand-up figures are played with at the small tables. Within the ring, the teaching-learning format relies primarily on infant-infant interaction with mothers supplying help and encouragement from their chairs outside the portayard. When the toddlers move to the tables, however, mothers maintain close physical contact. Supervision, help in fitting materials, verbal instructions, and looking at picture books together require mother's active participation.

During this period of development, mothers learn that the inner forces which propel toddlers from one stage of development to the next are the drive to become independent, the drive toward mastery of their environment, and the drive to fit in socially—to belong, to please, to become part of. They acknowledge the drive to become independent by encouraging their infants to participate in feeding, dressing, and bathing rituals without having unrealistic expectations of the baby's capabilities. The infant's drive toward mastery of his physical environment includes his continued mastery of eye-hand coordination skills, and facility in this area requires a variety of manipulative experiences and a teaching model which ensures success. Mothers are instructed to satisfy their infants' needs to please and to become part of the social environment by taking time to play with them as they master new skills and by rewarding them with their presence as well as with praise.

The following materials are given to the mothers for use in cooperative play sessions at home: table and chair set for fostering order and organization, rock-a-stack for discrimination of size, simple object pictures in hard-cover and cloth books for language development, large crayons and eighteen by twenty-four inch newsprint for fine motor control, a shape sorter box for discrimination of shape, pop beads and unifix cubes for fitting and taking apart, a threading clock and stringing beads for introduction to multi-operational learning tasks, and a top and pop-up box for cause and effect relationships.

NATURE OF PARENT INVOLVEMENT

The mothers' training model emphasizes mother as teacher and speaks to the belief that parents are the most potent force in determining the ultimate competency of their offspring. The model is based on the assumption that educators in the field of early childhood could and should train parents to maximize their role as teachers.

Since this intervention focused on adolescent mothers (sixteen years and younger) and their firstborn infants, recruitment in the postpartum unit of a large inner-city hospital was found to be highly effective. Virtually all young mothers feel some motivation to learn about "parenting" at the time their first child is born. Social history data reveal that most of the mothers are unmarried, living at home, and receiving welfare. Their return to school is facilitated by help provided within the extended family, and approximately 50 percent of these young mothers are back in school within three months after delivery. As a result, babies are often surrendered to the maternal grandmother for primary care, and we suspect that many of these young mothers view their participation in training classes as a means of more clearly establishing their role as mother, perhaps in competition with their own mothers.

Although only telephone contact is used as the follow-up procedure for ensuring participation after recruitment during the lying-in period, three out of four mothers join classes. Group identity, as evidenced by spontaneity in sharing and volunteered comments, is almost immediately established. Instructors, volunteers, and students participating in the classes attest to the mothers' interest in the content of the classes and the manner in which it is taught. The satisfactions a new mother experiences with a peer group of young mothers, the therapy provided through the sharing of common problems, the availability of adult teaching models, and the interest and concern extended toward her and her infant by attendant staff all serve to influence in positive ways her growth as a person and as a mother. We have, in fact, been obliged to continue follow-up classes—until infants are six months of age—for those mother-infant pairs in the service model who completed only the first series of eight classes.

STAFF DEVELOPMENT

A core staff of two full-time early childhood educators, one half-time pediatric nurse associate, and one full-time research technician trains and directs the activity of eight volunteers and five paraprofessionals.

Volunteers are nurses, educators, social workers, and psychologists who have visited the mothers' training classes and expressed an interest in learning how to administer the program. Typically, after a visit they receive their agency's approval to attend one or two series of ten weekly two-hour classes on the Infant Stimulation/Mothers' Training Project or one of our monthly all-day workshops. (Some volunteers received orientation and training at a four-day workshop conducted in August 1974.) Depending on their background and capabilities, these volunteers then assume one of three positions within the classroom structure: group leader-instructor, co-leader-facilitator, or observer-recorder. All receive weekly orientation on the material to be covered that week.

The five paraprofessionals are all graduates of the pilot eighteen-month mothers' training program. They also attend a series of twelve classes specifically designed to prepare them for employment in the project. Besides serving as catalysts in new mothers' training classes, they also work under the direction of a child development specialist as infant stimulators in one of five weekly daytime pediatric-clinic waiting-room programs for mothers and infants.

ADMINISTRATIVE CONSIDERATIONS

The Cincinnati Maternal and Infant Care Project funded our project in the amount of $55,000 for fiscal year 1974. The budget includes salaries for four full-time staff members and for five paraprofessionals employed on a part-time basis. Transportation expense (cab pools for mothers and infants attending classes) is also included.

Toys and educational materials and expenses incurred in carrying out research are provided through private grants and contracts (Andrew Jergens Foundation, Maternity Society, Ruth Lyons Fund, Cincinnati Public Schools) which have totalled $17,000 over the past two years. Technical assistance in the analysis of research data, office space and equipment, and all overhead expenses are shared by the University of Cincinnati College of Medicine, Department of Pediatrics—Newborn Division, and the Children's Hospital Research Foundation.

The research and demonstration focus of the pilot project has resulted in a service program for all adolescent mothers and their newborn infants delivered at CGH. The actual cost per mother-infant pair who attend weekly classes, beginning three weeks after delivery and continuing until the infant is six months old, is sixty-five dollars. This cost includes transportation to and from class and the toys and educational materials given to the mother.

FIGURE 1

UZGIRIS-HUNT ORDINAL SCALES
COMPOSITE SCORES

SIX- AND TWELVE-MONTH MEAN COMPOSITE TESTING SCORES
ON UZGIRIS-HUNT ORDINAL SCALES OF PSYCHOLOGICAL DE-
VELOPMENT FOR FOUR GROUPS OF MATCHED INFANTS. ANAL-
YSIS OF VARIANCE INDICATED A SIGNIFICANT DIFFERENCE
BETWEEN INFANTS (YOUNG AND OLD MOTHERS) IN CLASS
GROUPS AND INFANTS (BOTH YOUNG AND OLD MOTHERS) IN
HOME VISITING GROUPS AT THIS LEVEL. THE TREATMENT
EFFECT WAS PRIMARILY APPARENT IN YOUNG MOTHERS'
GROUPS.

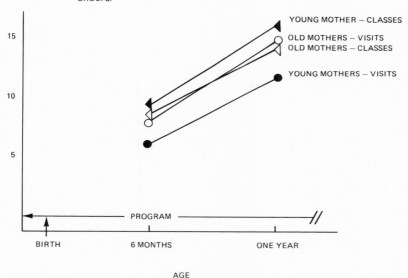

EVALUATION

In the pilot mothers' training program, infant testing data at twelve
months—Uzgiris-Hunt Infant Ordinal Scales of Psychological Development
and Bayley Infant Scales—indicated that infants of young mothers attending weekly classes performed significantly better than infants of young
mothers in the home-visited comparison group. This treatment effect was
not apparent in infants of slightly older and more mature mothers whose
infants performed equally well in class and home visited groups (Figures
1, 2, 3).

In our sample of forty-eight young (sixteen years and under) and old

58

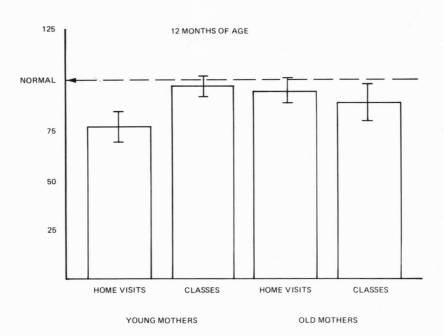

FIGURE 2

BAYLEY SCALE (MENTAL)

MEAN TWELVE-MONTH SCORE ON BAYLEY MENTAL SCALES FOR
EACH OF FOUR TREATMENT GROUPS. INFANTS OF YOUNG
MOTHERS IN HOME VISITED GROUP HAD MEAN MENTAL SCORE
OF SEVENTY-NINE, WHICH IS SIGNIFICANTLY LESS (P. 05) THAN
MEAN SCORE OF NINETY-NINE OBTAINED BY INFANTS OF
YOUNG MOTHERS IN CLASS GROUP. OTHER INTERGROUP DIF-
FERENCES ARE NOT SIGNIFICANT.

(eighteen years and older) mothers of firstborn infants, equally divided
into weekly class or monthly home-visited groups, only two sociological
variables negatively influenced infant performance. Infants of mothers
living alone performed less well than infants of mothers living within
extended families or with a husband ($p<.01$). Secondly, infants of mothers
categorized by program criteria as having *multiple problems* (lack of
family support, inability to utilize resources, low self-esteem, school drop-
out) performed less well than infants of mothers who were not so described ($p<.01$). In our total sample of forty-eight mother-infant pairs, ten
mothers met the program criteria for multiple problems and were evenly

FIGURE 3

BAYLEY SCORE (MOTOR)

MEAN TWELVE-MONTH SCORE ON BAYLEY MOTOR SCALES FOR
EACH OF FOUR TREATMENT GROUPS. INFANTS OF YOUNG
MOTHERS IN CLASS GROUP PERFORMED SIGNIFICANTLY BET-
TER (P.05) THAN THOSE IN HOME VISITING GROUP. MOTOR
SCORES OF THESE INFANTS WERE SIGNIFICANTLY BETTER
(P. 01) THAN THOSE OF INFANTS WITH OLDER MOTHERS WHO
ALSO ATTENDED CLASSES.

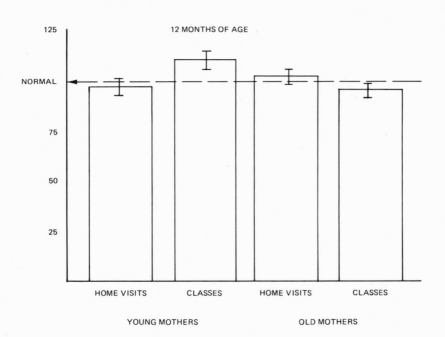

divided between class and home-visited groups as well as between the
young and old mother classifications. Two were white mothers.

It is interesting to note that in the subsequent scheduling of new
mothers' training classes, one out of four mothers recruited during the
lying-in period failed to attend classes. These mothers may be generally
described as having multiple problems and as difficult to motivate and
influence positively in the nurturing of their infants. This experience seems
to support the case for infant day-care programs if the infants of these
mothers are to thrive and achieve a measure of competence in life.

Our first year evaluation of forty-eight mother-infant pairs who were recruited at the postpartum unit of a large inner-city hospital and who participated in one of two intervention programs (weekly classes or monthly home visits) suggests that the mother-infant group approach is especially effective with high-risk, adolescent mothers. That the postpartum period appears to be the optimal recruitment time is evidenced by our continued success in recruiting adolescent mothers for participation in mother-infant classes. Further, the cost analysis of intervention favors the group approach.

FUTURE PLANS

Delivering an educational intervention program for mothers and infants under the umbrella of a large university medical center has several advantages, not the least of which has been our impact on the traditional way health care services have been defined and provided. Comprehensive health services in Cincinnati have now begun to include infant stimulation and training in "parenting." Pediatric clinic waiting rooms throughout the city are presently being transformed into stimulating learning environments for parents and children. Practicum experiences provided in our mother-infant classes to professionals from many disciplines have resulted in innovative ways of expanding mental health, school, and medical services. Public health nurses who routinely visit each mother in the home after delivery have begun to expand their services to include postnatal classes for adolescent mothers and their infants. Two health department clinics, recognizing their special needs as well as the mothers' responsiveness to the group approach, have initiated monthly cluster visits for adolescent mothers and their infants. Two high schools plan to initiate within-school mother-infant classes as part of their curriculums. Two private agencies serving middle-class clientele have begun postnatal mother-infant classes. Many of the professionals involved in intervention programs for mothers and infants have banded together to form an organization called United Services for Effective Parenting (USEP). In-service training, sharing of educational materials, joint purchase of toys, and a central referral system characterize this cooperative effort to serve high-risk mothers and infants more effectively.

Our future plans are to continue to assist agencies in implementing educational programs, including ten area programs begun by the State Department of Vocational Education, for high risk mother-infant pairs. We intend to begin involving young fathers with adolescent mothers and their infants in weekly classes, and a male neonatologist will assist in the leadership of the first group. We would also like to replicate our program model with low birthweight infants and their mothers and would initiate such a program while the infants were in the intensive care nursery.

The appeal of our project has opened doors in changing the early-education focus from remediation to prevention of learning handicaps. Identification of high risk mother-infant pairs within the newborn unit of a hospital greatly facilitates recruitment. Perhaps most significantly, our experience suggests that creative medical personnel welcome the opportunity to become involved in educational intervention.

ACKNOWLEDGMENTS

In giving credit to the many people who have participated in the development of the mothers' training model, I am forever indebted to the fifteen mother-infant pairs who were part of the first mothers' training program which was carried out at the University of Illinois in Champaign-Urbana from 1967-1969. These mothers convinced me that it was possible to train parents to become effective teachers of their children. As the program was transplanted into the pediatric setting of a large university medical center, Drs. James Sutherland, Martin Saidleman, William Keenan, Jean Steichen, and Ross Parke became prime movers. And, without any form of federal funding to support our research efforts, we are grateful to the following professional volunteers: social workers Mary Beavan, Barbara Roder, Ruth Goldberg, Philip Schwartz; nurses Judy Noble, Debbie Wilkins, Pat Zappin, Gale Ossenbeck, Pam Poth, Cheryl Ackerhausen; educators Liz Hattemer, Ginny Paine, Sheila Hoffman, Marta Stegman, Sue Heilman, Sr. Marie Christopher, Sr. Mary Eileen. And, lastly I am personally indebted to Dr. J. McVicker Hunt from the University of Illinois for all the personal help and encouragement he has provided during the past five years. A sequential learning program for infants and toddlers and the mothers' training model are the result of my productive association with Dr. Hunt.

BIBLIOGRAPHY

Badger, E. *Infant and toddler learning program.* Paoli, Pennsylvania: McGraw-Hill Early Learning, Instructo Corporation, 1971.

Badger, E. A mothers' training program — The road to a purposeful existence. *Children,* 1971, 18, 51, 168-173.

Badger, E. Mothers' training program — A sequel article. *Children Today,* 1972, 1, 3, 7-12.

Badger, E., Elsass, S., and Sutherland, J. Mother training as a means of accelerating childhood development in a high risk population. Paper presented at Society for Pediatric Research, Washington, D.C., May 2, 1974.

Badger, E. *Mother's guide to early learning,* Illustrated, 60 page, easy-to-read parents' companion to the Infant and Toddler Learning Programs. Available from: Wabash Area Parent Child Center, P. O. Box 189, Mt. Carmel, Illinois, 62863.

Badger, E. *Development of language.* Illustrated, 15 page, easy-to-read parents' guide to sequential development of language during the first two years of life. Available from: University of Cincinnati College of Medicine, Department of Pediatrics, 231 Bethesda Avenue, Cincinnati, Ohio, 45267.

Brazelton, T. Berry. *Infants and mothers: Difference in development.* New York: Dell Publishing Co., Inc., 1972.

CHAPTER 5

Preventing Mental Retardation Through Family Rehabilitation

Howard L. Garber

In the early 1960s, the University of Wisconsin's Research and Training Center in Mental Retardation, under the direction of Professor Rick Heber, established a research effort focused on the type of mental retardation commonly associated with the economically disadvantaged. This form of retardation, referred to as "cultural-familial" or "socio-cultural," is the mildest and also the most prevalent of all forms. Of all individuals defined or classified as mentally retarded, nearly 80 percent fall into the cultural-familial category.

The initial effort for the study involved developing essential information, previously not readily available, on the characteristics of the disadvantaged (low socio-economic status) population in which an excessive prevalence of the mild form of mental retardation exists (IQ range of 50 to 75). Few other contemporary social problems have stirred so much controversy, often expressed with more emotion than reason, as the etiology of this form of retardation. Its subtlety has plagued research efforts. Since no gross pathology of behavior is manifest, there is considerable speculation as to its etiology. Unfortunately, the most obvious characteristic of cultural-familial retardation, as mentioned, is its high prevalence among the low-SES (socio-economic status) populations, which usually include large numbers of racial and cultural minority groups. This connection is

HOWARD GARBER is a Research Associate at the Waisman Center on Mental Retardation and Human Development at the University of Wisconsin in Madison. Infant intervention is one of his primary interests.

especially unfortunate, because the obvious characteristics of these groups, together with their social and economic plight, have traditionally distracted research efforts. The result is a tendency to see all individuals with similar epidemiological characteristics as having the same mental score, and, further, to assume that this score is indeed a valid measure of not only one individual's potential but also the potential of all members of the group to which he belongs.

In our work at Wisconsin, we committed ourselves to the examination of the epidemiological characteristics of the severely disadvantaged. We began in the early 1960s by examining the characteristics of a population at *high risk* for mental retardation. The initial effort to develop information on the characteristics of the low socio-economic status individual who is mildly retarded was facilitated by the establishment of the High-Risk Population Laboratory. (See Heber and Garber, 1975, for a more detailed discussion of epidemiology.)

The High-Risk Population Laboratory is in an area of Milwaukee, Wisconsin which had previously been found to have an extremely high prevalence of retardation, and which we began to monitor by surveys. Although this area comprised only aboubt 2.5 percent of the city's population, it yielded approximately 33 percent of the total number of children identified in school as "educable mentally retarded." Furthermore, according to U.S. Census Bureau data, the tracts comprising this area were in the lowest category in median educational level and income, and in the highest categories of population density per living unit (of percent houses rated as dilapidated) and of unemployment.

The purpose of the High-Risk Population Laboratory was to provide information for the early detection of the cultural-familial retarded. Because of its mildness and lack of obvious pathology in the early years, cultural-familial retardation is generally undetected until school age. With the kind of information we hoped to gain from our surveys, a prospective longitudinal study, with major emphasis on prevention, could be made of cultural-familial mental retardation. This approach was in contrast to traditional research efforts which were based mainly on retrospective data in which treatment was remediation.

Two striking characteristics of the low SES population with a high incidence of mental retardation emerged from the survey data (Heber, Dever, and Conry, 1968). First, there was a differential course of intellectual development for children born to mothers with different IQ levels. The offspring of mothers with IQs below 80 declined to a mean retarded level of IQ performance with increasing age, while the performance of the offspring of mothers with IQs above 80 remained stable and within the normal range. Second, the offspring of the retarded mothers were found to be in the normal IQ range when they were tested during the infancy period and began the marked decline after about age three. Our data suggest that the lower the maternal IQ, the greater the probability of the children scoring low on intelligence tests, particularly the children of mothers with IQs below 80. Although the trend to decline in measured intelligence is accepted as typical for children in severely disadvantaged environments, our data indicate that it is restricted to certain children from certain specifiable families, and that these families can be identified by low maternal intelligence.

The strategy for our study was based on these data. Our hypothesis was that we could approach the prevention of socio-cultural mental retardation by attempting to rehabilitate the family rather than simply the individual retarded adult. We now have a technique by which we could select families at high risk for mental retardation on the basis of maternal intelligence and with which we could initiate a program to study the possibility of preventing retardation in the new offspring of these families.

PROJECT DESIGN

As babies were born in our study area, trained surveyors employed by the University of Wisconsin Survey Research Center contacted the family within a few weeks of each birth and completed a family history questionnaire which included a vocabulary screening test administered to the mother. Those mothers falling below a cut-off score on the vocabulary test were given a full-scale WAIS (Wechsler Adult Intelligence Scale) by a trained psychometrist. A maternal IQ on the WAIS of less than 75 was the selection criterion used in accumulating a sample of forty families. These forty families were assigned to either the "experimental" or "control" condition. An additional selection criterion was that the sample be restricted to black families. The basis for this decision was: (1) according to 1960 census data, black families residing in the study area were less mobile than white families (a suggestion that attrition would be less of a problem with black families); and (2) we desired to minimize potential culture- and race-related problems within the group of experimental families.

Because of the design requirement that intervention be initiated as early in infancy as possible, the sample of 40 families in which the mother met the WAIS selection criterion could not first be accumulated and then randomly assigned to the experimental and control groups. Our projections indicated that screening procedures would identify about three families a month who met the criterion and thus a little better than one year would be required to accumulate the full sample. In actual fact, our projections were somewhat off, and a total of eighteen months was actually required.

Furthermore, because of such logistical considerations as preparing the infant intervention staff, arranging transportation of infants to the infant center, etc., we decided to assign infants to experimental and control groups on a monthly basis rather than on an alternate one-by-one basis, although in some cases it required two months to produce an increment of three or four for assignment. Although this procedure constituted a deviation from strictly random assignment, statistical analysis showed no significant differences between the two groups in all measures, such as birth weight and height, recorded abnormality of delivery or condition of the infant at birth, marital status of family, economic status, and number of siblings, present and known at time of birth.

The design of the Milwaukee project for the experimental group called for a comprehensive family intervention effort beginning in the home. The experimental program was composed of two components: (1) the infant and early childhood stimulation program and (2) a maternal rehabilitation program. Intervention into the experiential environment of the experimental infants began as soon as was feasible after birth (six months) and continued to the age of regular school entry (CA* six years). Its objective was to provide experiences that were potentially lacking in the natural environment of the "high-risk" infant which could facilitate the development of cognitive skills.

MATERNAL REHABILITATION PROGRAM

One of the major purposes of the Family Rehabilitation Program was to change the behavior of the low-SES, low-IQ mother within the home and within the community. In the past, a major obstacle to this kind of effort was the attitude of the mentally retarded mothers themselves. Feelings of hostility and suspicion toward social agencies and a sense of despair (social and economic) pervaded their lives. We designed an experimental rehabilitation program for these mothers which included: (1) vocational information and counseling; (2) occupational training in areas such as laundry, janitorial work, and food preparation; (3) remedial academic education; (4) motivation training; and (5) training in budgeting and home management.

The occupational training program utilized two large private nursing homes in Milwaukee. The choice of the nursing homes as sites for training was made because of the appropriate job skill areas represented in these facilities, the availability of professional staff with some understanding of

* Chronological Age

rehabilitation problems, and the employment opportunities available in nursing homes and other chronic-care facilities. Following this initial training phase, which enabled a number of mothers to find employment, we shifted emphasis to the educational phase of the program, which was carried out during the evening at the center. A remedial educational program was designed and taught by the program staff. The basic academic curriculum emphasized reading, writing, and arithmetic. In addition, the curriculum included home economics, community-oriented social studies, interpersonal relations, and home management.

Essentially, the maternal rehabilitation program appears to have been quite successful to date. We evaluated its effectiveness by using a series of measures to provide information about the differences in home life, attitudes, self-concept, etc., between the experimental and control mothers; we also conducted a study of the way in which these mothers interacted with their children. For example, the experimental mothers encouraged reciprocal communication between themselves and their infants. The result of this attitude change is reflected in the experimental mothers' greater tendency to engage in verbally informative behaviors rather than non-task oriented physical behaviors (shown by the control mothers and by the experimental mothers at the beginning of the program). In contrast, the attitudes of the control mothers showed no relationship to the behaviors observed when they were interacting with their children. We also found that the experimental mothers showed a greater tendency toward an internal locus of control, an indication that they felt more in control of their environment. Such feelings of control are transmitted to the child, whose self-confidence is thereby enhanced.

Such changes in the mothers' attitudes and self-concepts are especially significant because they signal an increase in the mothers' sensitivity to their own needs and the needs of their families and an increased receptivity to the suggestions of respected and responsible outsiders. It is now more likely that these parents will make use of community resources. In other words, it seems that, as a result of the long-term rehabilitation of families with a retarded mother, these families are more motivated to seek out, participate in, and profit from the rehabilitation resources in the community and, further, are more sensitive to the nutritional and health needs of their children.

We have recently retested all the mothers in both the experimental and control groups. A preliminary analysis of the data indicated no significant change from the original testing nearly eight years before, even with a mean positive increase of about five points. However, whereas our determination of the literacy rate showed both groups to be comparable originally (35 percent vs. 22 percent), these groups are now considerably different (experimental at 60 percent and control at 38 percent). But both groups' mean reading levels are very low (Grade level: experimental at 4.2 and control at 3.4). Obviously, there are major implications, in this regard, for the success in school of the offspring of such mothers. What is also obvious is the tremendous help needed by such families, which when given (as in the case of the Family Rehabilitation Project's effort for the last seven or more years), can have a tremendous impact.

While the actual vocational rehabilitation program was conducted only during the first years of the project, we have continued parent support and the counseling program to the present. A full-time parent coordinator has maintained individual contact with the families. She has counseled them in the areas of nutrition, preventive medicine (e.g., inoculations), medical insurance, legal and social problems, etc. Upon the mother's request, the parent-coordinator has attended public school conferences about older siblings, and has talked to landlords and to social service workers. It has also been the parent-coordinator's responsibility to provide the parents with constant feedback about their child's learning performance and behavior at the center. She has arranged the biannual open house and parent-teacher conferences. The position of the parent-coordinator has been vital to the effectiveness of the whole intervention program. She has mediated problems between parents, between parents and staff, and between the children and their parents. But most important, she has always been available to aid the parents during critical periods.

THE INFANT STIMULATION PROJECT

The program was designed, basically, to facilitate the intellectual and social development of very young children through a comprehensive educational intervention program beginning early in life. The program intervened early (infants began between three and six months of age); it intervened intensively (children attended from 9 a.m. to 4 p.m. each weekday on a year-round schedule for their first six years); it intervened relevantly (it was designed specifically for the "high-risk" children it was serving).

Physical plant. The project was located in several sites over the years. First, we renovated a large fourteen-room house in the inner city. This was particularly suited to very young children because of the many small areas which allowed for more intimate teacher-child contact and many places for nap time. Later, when the children were older and more mobile, we rented space in a Salvation Army facility. This provided open space (inside and out) for gross motor activities, as well as several small rooms for individual and small group instruction. The entire program was then moved to a leased school facility, located adjacent to one of the inner city's churches. This building had six classrooms, a gymnasium, a stage, a lunch room and kitchen, and office space.

Staff. At the onset of the infant program, we chose to employ a paraprofessional staff. The persons chosen were, in our judgment, language-facile, affectionate people who had had some experience with infants or young children. The majority of these "teachers" resided in the same general neighborhood as the children and therefore shared their cultural milieu. The teachers ranged in age from eighteen to forty-five, with most in their mid-twenties. Their educational experience ranged from eighth grade to one year of college. The teachers were both black and white.

The teachers' responsibilities were quite varied, and training for their duties required a combination of instructional staff meetings, on-the-job training, and in-service programs. A teacher was assigned to each new infant whose family was enrolled in the program. Each infant's teacher was given help in organizing her day in order to provide for the infant's physical care and instruction, which included activities appropriate for that child. Each teacher was observed and evaluated frequently by the curriculum supervisors. Issues related specifically to a teacher, such as choice of activity, attitude toward the child, behavior problems, etc., were discussed privately with her. General problem areas were discussed with the entire group at regular staff meetings or during the annual three-day seminar.

The teacher of an infant was responsible for establishing the initial rapport with the family. This was done during a brief period, ranging from two to eight weeks, when the teacher worked with her child in the home until the mother expressed enough confidence in the teacher to allow the child to go to the center. The child remained with her primary teacher throughout the first year.

The teacher was responsible for her infant's total care, including feeding and bathing, cuddling and soothing, reporting and recording general health, organizing the learning environment, and implementing the educational program. Within the context of the educational program, the teacher was expected to follow and expand upon a suggested set of activities. Her job was to make these activities interesting, exciting, and varied. She was instructed on how to evaluate and report the child's progress, and how to pinpoint areas of apparent difficulty.

The teacher-pupil ratios varied with the age levels of the children, but allowances were made for the special needs of the individual child. Under most circumstances, the infant remained with a teacher on a one-to-one basis up to twelve months, at which time another teacher and child were paired with him to encourage the expansion of relationships. When the children were around fifteen months old, a transition period began during which two children were assigned to one teacher. When they reached the age of eighteen months, small groups began to be formed so that by about twenty-four months all children of the same age level (about a five-month span) were grouped together with enough teachers to provide a 1:3 teacher-pupil ratio. During the small group learning periods, the teacher-pupil ratio may have been 1:2, 1:3, or 1:4, depending upon the ages and the abilities of the children. Within each age group, behavioral and educational evaluations were made by the teachers, the teacher supervisor, and curriculum supervisors during conferences in which decisions were made on whether or not to regroup children, provide individual instruction, or make curriculum changes.

Educational program. The design of the curriculum and its implementation has been the responsibility of Ms. Caroline Hoffman and Ms. Susan Harrington. The general goal they established for the educational program was to provide an environment and a set of experiences which would allow each child to develop in his potential intellectually, as well as socially, emotionally, and physically. The program emphasized the development of language and cognitive skills and was designed to maintain a positive and responsive learning environment for the children. The specific focus was on those skill areas (e.g., language, problem-solving, and achievement motivation) in which the mildly retarded and severely disadvantaged have often been found deficient.

The general educational program is best described as a program with a cognitive-language orientation implemented through a planned environment utilizing informal prescriptive teaching techniques. Translated into action, "prescriptive teaching" means: (1) direct observations of the child's strengths, weaknesses, and preferences, (2) gearing tasks and experiences specifically to each child, and (3) evaluating the effect of the task or experience on the child.

Hoffman and Harrington have outlined five major principles that they used as a guide in developing a curriculum that extends from early infancy to school entrance:

(1) Learning is a developmental process that occurs as a function of the interaction between maturation and experience.

(2) The design of an educational program requires knowledge of (a) child development, (b) predicted deficits in the study population, and (c) the children's current levels of functioning.

(3) The program must be responsive to the needs of the individual child.

(4) Comprehensive programming recognizes that the individual child requires support for all growth areas, including the child's social-emotional, physical, and intellectual development.

(5) A core of teachers should be maintained throughout the program, which must in turn be responsive to the needs of the teachers.

With these guidelines, a program which emphasized both language and cognitive growth was implemented. Language was considered the basis of social communication as well as the key to the higher mental processes and a major influence on an individual's interpretation of his environment. Throughout the program, all tasks or experiences were presented to the child with emphasis on the development of receptive and expressive language skills, and particularly on the "cognitive use of language," i.e., those skills which enable children to think creatively and critically and to reason. The more formal aspect of the language program used, among other tools, the Peabody Language Development Kit (levels #P and L). It is particularly well suited for use by paraprofessional teachers. The Peabody program stresses overall oral language development and concentrates on the cognitive aspects of language.

The educational program's second emphasis was on cognitive development. Hoffman and Harrington felt the curriculum should be designed to provide those kinds of cognitive experiences that will not only allow the child to incorporate, integrate, and refine various bits of information, but, more important, will enable him to act spontaneously and creatively in changing situations. The more formal aspects of concern for cognitive development were treated in a mathematics and problem-solving curriculum. This curriculum developed a complex of tasks based on certain cognitive skills, e.g., classification, association, seriation, analysis, matching, etc.

During the infancy period, the curriculum was divided into three main areas of development: social-emotional growth, perceptual-motor growth, and cognitive-language growth. In the preschool years, the emphasis was on the cognitive language area, which was broken down into the overlapping units of reading, language, and math-problem solving, with perceptual-motor functioning and social-emotional growth underlying all areas of the curriculum. Each teacher became a specialist in one of the three curriculum areas. The children spent two, half-hour periods each day with each of three teachers in small group, direct learning activities. They also participated in child-directed activities in an open environment where they were given the opportunity to use and expand the concepts presented in the small groups. The balance between teacher- and child-directed activities provided the opportunity for the children to generalize and practice newly learned skills.

A third emphasis of the program was a concern for the personal development of the children. Although language was emphasized as a tool for processing information as well as for communication, and although cognitive development was emphasized to enhance creative thinking as well as to provide the child with a repertoire of responses, it was recognized that the force necessary to make this system work was the desire to utilize these skills—i.e., motivation. There was an attempt to develop achievement motivation both by designing tasks and by creating an atmosphere which would develop maximum interest, provide success experiences, provide supportive and corrective feedback from responsive adults, and gradually increase the child's responsibility for task completion.

ASSESSMENT OF DEVELOPMENT

In order to assess the effects of the kind of comprehensive intervention in the natural environment of the infant and his retarded mother, an intensive schedule of measurements was undertaken. The schedule for infants included: medical evaluations; standard Gesell and Piagetian experimental measures of the development of infant behavior; standardized tests of general intelligence, including the Stanford-Binet, the Wechsler Preschool and Primary Scale of Intelligence (WPPSI), and the Wechsler Intelligence Scale for Children (WISC); an array of experimental learning tasks, including probability matching and discrimination; measures of mother-child interaction; and a variety of measures of language development, including the Illinois Test of Psycholinguistic Abilities (ITPA) and several research instruments concerned with various aspects of linguistic development.

Both the experimental and control infants were on an identical measurement schedule which for infants during the preschool program, was keyed to each child's birth date. For infants from ages six to twenty-four months, assessments were scheduled on a bi-monthly basis; after the child reached the age of twenty-four months, testing was done every three weeks. The particular measure administered at a given session depended upon the predetermined schedule of measures for that age level. Each test or task was administered to both the experimental and control infants by the same person. The testers, however, were not involved in any component of the children's educational program. The testers were both white and black.

The Gesell Developmental Schedules revealed the first significant difference in performance between the two groups of children. In tests administered through the fourteen months, the two groups responded comparably on the four schedules: motor, adaptive, language, and personal-social. At eighteen months, the control group fell three to four months below the experimental group, although it still performed close to Gesell norms. At twenty-two months, the experimental group scores were from four-and-a-half to six months in advance of the control group on all four schedules, while the control group had fallen below the Gesell norms on the adaptive and language schedules.

The divergence in performance was maintained beyond the twenty-four month mark. At twenty-four months, the groups began Cattell and Stanford-Binet testing. From twenty-four months to seventy-two months, the mean IQ of the experimental group remained more than 20 points higher than that of the control group. The mean IQ of the experimental group across all testings between twenty-four and seventy-two months was 123.4, in comparison to the control mean IQ of 94.4 for the same period of time. At the mean age of seventy-two months, the experimental group's mean IQ was 120.7 (SD = 11.2), whereas that of the control group was 87.2 (SD = 12.8), a difference of over 30 IQ points. (These mean levels of IQ performance have been substantiated by an independent testing service using a "double bind" procedure.)

The apparent trend of the control group toward declining IQ was comparable to the performance data obtained in our original survey work. Also, we sampled all of the siblings from both the experimental and control groups and found that their IQ performance had also tended to decline with increasing age. For the experimental group, however, it appeared that this decline was prevented.

We have only recently finished retesting all of the siblings from both the experimental and control groups. Combined performance data indicated that the trend to declining IQ was maintained, but differentially, in both groups. The experimental and control siblings between the ages of three and seven years had a comparable mean IQ of 83 and 81.3 (respectively). However, the mean IQ performance for the control siblings continued to decline between the ages of ten to fourteen years and beyond to a mean of 75.6, whereas the experimental siblings' mean IQ discontinued the decline and remained at 87.6. Although further analysis remains to be done, this differential in performance suggested a positive effect throughout the family as a result of the parent's and target child's participation in the experimental program (see, e.g., Klaus and Gray, 1970).

In summary, the performance data from the standardized tests of intelligence indicated that we have prevented the relative decline in intellectual development that is now seen in the control group, and that was found in the siblings (although differentially) of both groups and in the original survey sample.

As outlined earlier, our assessment program included several other measures besides IQ tests. When we began our assessment program, we wanted more comprehensive information about cognitive growth than can be derived from IQ tests. When the primary concern of an early education program is cognitive development, IQ tests of individuals in the program are not adequate measures of the program's efficacy. In particular, such tests are more sensitive to changes caused by certain kinds of educational training programs than they are to the development of the various response systems in the child. We wanted information on response patterns or behavior styles and on the way a child's simple choice may reveal his general response tendencies and his ability to select and order incoming stimulation. In addition, we wanted more comprehensive information about language skills than we could obtain from the IQ tests or standardized language measures.

In the learning-performance tasks, such as color-form and probability matching and oddity discrimination, the experimental group was superior to the control group on all testings between the ages of two-and-a-half and six years. However, the more important aspect of the differences in performance was the development of more sophisticated and more consistent response behaviors by the experimental children. Generally, the experimental children utilized a response strategy which demonstrated their tendency to use strategies or hypotheses-testing behavior and their sensitiveness to feedback information from their response behavior. The control children, on the other hand, showed a marked tendency to response stereotypy, often persevered in their responses with no attempt to use a strategy; also, they tended to be passive and unenthusiastic in their response behavior. This early learning performance has major implications for the future: for the experimental children, this approach to problem-solving should be facilitative, while the behavior style of the control children will interfere with their ability to learn and perform.

Our second area of assessment was language development. The first significant difference between the two groups in language performance, measured on the language scale of the Gesell Developmental Schedule, appeared at the age of eighteen months. By twenty-two months, the experimental children were over four months ahead of the norm and six months ahead of the control children. This trend of differential language development continued throughout the program. We used several instruments, including an analysis of free speech samples, a sentence repetition test, a grammatical comprehension test, a test of morphology, and the ITPA. On all of these language tests, the performance of the experimental children was superior to that of the control children. In fact, they demonstrated an accelerated process of learning, built perhaps on their initially higher level of language performance. According to the Grammatical Comprehension Test, for example, the *rate* at which grammatical structures were acquired by the experimental group at the age of three to three-and-a-half was not approximated by the control children until they were over five years old. This difference in the rate at which grammatical structures were acquired had less to do with dialect factors than with the ability to understand concepts, such as negation and plurality, and relationships, such as the spatial relationships indicated by prepositions, and the sameness or reciprocity of actor and object, as expressed by reflexive and reciprocal pronouns.

Another way of looking beyond test scores and into the quality of performance was to examine the children's errors on the tests. This was done with the Sentence Repetition Tests, in which all responses were recorded on tape and transcribed. While it may be argued that a child's ability to imitate a standard English sentence accurately is influenced by his familiarity with standard English, we found, from the errors made by both the experimental and the control children, that there was in fact a very pronounced qualitative difference in control of syntax between the two groups. The experimental children generally made minor mistakes, such as dropping past tense or plural markers, or inserting a relative conjunction where it had been deleted in the original sentence. The first type of error is closely bound to dialect influence; the second (e.g., "The cat *that* the dog chased ran away" for "The cat the dog chased ran away") is an error only in a very technical sense. It is in fact an indication that the sentence has been understood, and that the child has provided his own verbal cue to clarify the sentence to himself. The errors made by the control group were of a sharply different nature: they were largely omissions or substitutions that destroyed or radically altered the structure of the original sentence and gave no indication that the sentence had been understood. The scores on the test, therefore, only gave an indication of the lower bounds of a child's linguistic ability. (See Reyes, Heber, and Garber, 1974).

The ITPA was administered to all children at four and a half and six and a half years of age. The ITPA results, like the results of our other measures, showed a difference in performance between the Experimental and Control children. The differences (between the two groups) that had been found when the children were four and a half were still present when the children were tested at six and a half. The Experimental children performed six months above their mean CA while the Control children were eleven months below their mean CA. The psycholinguistic quotient (PLQ) for the Experimental children was 107.8 as against 87.3 for the Control children—a difference of 20.5 points (see Flynn, Garber and

Heber, 1974).

We could describe the language behavior of the experimental children as expressive, verbally fluent, and (according to the ITPA) linguistically sophisticated. They spoke their own dialect and were proud of their own speech; yet their performance was developmentally advanced on sophisticated tests of the English language. Our experimental children had help in something that transcended problems of dialect and included skills other than learning to produce acceptable sounds. They had help at a critical period of their growth in learning to perceive and express relationships on a verbal level and in processing linguistic information efficiently. While the children in the control group might, at any time, learn the same things the experimental children have already learned, the experimental children entered school better equipped with the language skills that they needed for further learning.

One other area of research which supports our other findings on the efficacy of intensive early cognitive stiumulation should be mentioned. We carefully examined mother-child interaction by using some of the techniques of Hess and Shipman (1968). In the mother-child interaction, most sophisticated behavior, such as the initiation of problem-solving behavior by verbal clues and verbal prods or the organization of tasks with respect to goals in problem-solving situations, is done by the mother. If the mother has a low IQ, however, the interaction is often more physical, less organized and less informative to the child than when the mother's IQ is higher.

We found more information was transmitted in the experimental dyads than in the control dyads, and that the increased transmission was a function of the quality of the experimental child's verbal behavior. The experimental children supplied more information verbally and initiated more verbal communication than the control dyads. The children in the experimental dyads took responsibility for guiding the flow of information and for providing most of the verbal information and direction. The mothers of both dyads showed little difference in their teaching ability during the testing sessions. However, in the experimental dyads, the children structured the interaction sessions either by their questioning or by teaching their mothers. Also, the experimental mothers appeared to be imitating some of the behaviors of their children. Consequently, they used more positive verbal reinforcement and more verbal responses. This finding suggests that the child can become the "educational engineer" in the dyad when there is a very low IQ, low verbal mother.

In order to assess the effectiveness of our early intervention program, we could ask, "What is the efficacy of the cognitive stimulation program?" From our data, it can be seen that there is not simply a difference in IQ levels but substantial differences in the language development between the two groups of children. Our findings to date are consistent with other early education programs in that the experimental children have shown considerable gains in IQ; we also found, however, that there were substantive changes in the intellectual structure of the children. This finding is critical because these children could expect little help from their families once they were in school.

These data summarize the present differences in development between the experimental and the control children, as well as those between their mothers. The present data in all areas of performance measured clearly indicate the superiority of the experimental group. Any ultimate evaluation, of course, must be based on the performance of these children as they move through the educational system. We are encoraged by the preliminary progress of those children from the experimental group who have completed first grade; final interpretations of the results, however, will be put off until more members of the group have reached this point.

In conclusion, the use of comprehensive rehabilitation of high-risk families must be deemed a successful approach to the prevention of mental retardation. This study, the Milwaukee Project, has in its approximately twelve years of operation produced three major findings which could be made operational:

1. The primary focus of this study has been the subpopulation of the mildly retarded group, known as the Cultural-Familial Mentally Retarded (CFMR), which is highly prevalent among certain low SES subpopulations. Discovery of the CFMR individual has generally been restricted to older individuals, since this form of retardation is so mild during the early years that younger individuals have remained undetected. So far, efforts to prevent CFMR have been hampered because there have been few opportunities for prospective investigations. The technique of early detection permitted us to study individuals who were not mentally retarded when very young but, because of certain epidemiological characteristics, ran a *high risk* of being retarded when they became older. Furthermore, our technique for the detection and discovery of the high-risk family represented a major breakthrough for the rehabilitation of certain low SES families because it permitted more equitable and more effective distribution of government resources and movement of social services among target families.

2. The rehabilitation effort of the Family Rehabilitation Study effectively changed the mother of the high-risk child into a more sensitive individual who became concerned for her family and for herself. Previous efforts at rehabilitation of the high-risk, low-SES, CFMR family evaluated the efficacy of their efforts in a superficial manner, since they had not investigated significant changes in the underlying life process of their

78

clients. Our research showed changes in the lives of the clients—both in their value system and in their family behavior system. The use of comprehensive family rehabilitation, remediation, and crisis consultation effected these changes in these families.

3. The use of the early and intensive stimulative and educational intervention, it appears, can successfully prevent mental retardation in the offspring of mentally retarded mothers and high-risk families by the time a child reaches school age. Major differences between treated children and untreated children appeared, not only in intellectual performance, but in behavior styles, learning performance, and language development.

Furthermore, as a result of the educational effort with the children from these target families, a major curriculum program was developed for use with similar populations of children. It is hoped that this program will be effective in facilitating both cognitive and social-emotional development.

Obviously, a continuing concern of the Family Rehabilitation Project is the status of these original project families—especially the children—during the coming years. Post-project follow-up evaluations have been planned and will be implemented in the coming months. We have also planned a comprehensive medical evaluation of all the children, and we are attempting to enlist the cooperation of the public schools in implementing a major analysis of peer and sibling academic performance. Compared to that of our target children, the performance of peers and siblings in similar environments represents an important category of data.

BIBLIOGRAPHY

Flynn, M., Garber, H., and Heber, R. Measuring differential language development in preschool age disadvantaged children with the Illinois Test of Psycholinguistic Abilities. Madison, Wisconsin: Research and Training Center in Mental Retardation, University of Wisconsin, 1974.

Heber, R., Dever, R., and Conry, J. The influence of environmental and genetic variables on intellectual development. In H. J. Prehm, L. A. Hamerlynck, and J. E. Crosson (Eds.), *Behavioral research in mental retardation.* Eugene, Oregon: University of Oregon, 1968.

Heber, R., and Garber, H. The Milwaukee Project: A study of the use of family intervention to prevent cultural-familial mental retardation. In B. Z. Friedlander, G. M. Sterritt, and G. E. Kirk (Eds,), *Exceptional infant.* (Volume 3: Assessment and Intervention). New York: Brunner/Mazel, 1975.

Hess, R., and Shipman, V. Maternal influences upon early learning: The cognitive environment of urban preschool children. In R. D. Hess and R. M. Ball, *Early education.* Chicago: Aldine, 1968.

Klaus, R., and Gray, S. Early Training Project: A seventh year report. Mimeograph, 1970.

Reyes, E. V., Garber, H., and Heber, R. Developmental differences in language as measured by a sentence repetition test. Madison, Wisconsin: Research and Training Center in Mental Retardation, University of Wisconsin, 1974.

CHAPTER 6

The Children's Center and the Family Development Research Program

Alice S. Honig

PROGRAM HISTORY AND
DESCRIPTION OF THE PRESENT PROGRAM

More than a decade ago (1964) the Children's Center (a school and day care center for infants, toddlers, and, later preschoolers) was founded by Dr. Bettye Caldwell under a grant from the Office of Child Development. At its inception, this program was conceptualized as one that could help prevent culturally determined mental retardation in children at risk. Indeed, from time to time, handicapped infants and toddlers were accepted into the program.

The Children's Center, housed in a new trailer and an old stucco house, met several challenging goals during the course of five pioneer years. One was the development of a warm, nurturing, and skilled staff that met the needs of infants and very young children in group care, and another was the creation of a "curriculum" for babies.

Children who attended this program for two years showed encouraging gains in cognitive functioning. Yet cognitive scores tended to decline as the children moved into the public school system. These findings, plus the experiences gained in the initial program, provided a seedbed for a second

---

ALICE S. HONIG is an Associate Professor in the College of Human Development at Syracuse University. Her major professional interests are infant development, parent involvement, preschool education, early language development, and program assessment.

Dr. J. Ronald Lally has directed the Family Development Research Program (FDRP) for the past six years. Dr. Lally placed the program's major emphasis on family development through home visitation of low-income families served by the project, which was also funded by the Office of Child Development. In addition, the Syracuse University Children's Center provided developmental day care, from six to sixty months for the first- or second-born target children of the families served. For two years (or until funds became available to keep children in the center after the age of three years) infants "graduating" from the project attended the Syracuse University Early Childhood Education Center, directed by Dr. Margaret Lay, until they reached public school age. Families in all cases continued to receive home visits until their children entered public schools.

Funding for new generations of infants was terminated in 1973. With the second grant, 108 families were served. None of the mothers were graduated from high school at the time the infants they enrolled in the program were born; and 85 percent of the households consisted of one-parent families. Energetic attempts were made to preserve ethnic balance in the program. However, differential attrition resulted in a predominantly black population. Many of the children graduated to kindergarten; and although fifty children from three to five years of age remain in the Children's Center, funding will not be available for this aspect of the program in the future.

The broad scope of the Family Development Research Program placed it in that category which Dr. Caldwell dubbed "omnibus models." A full complement of nutrition, health, safety, and child development services; information; and skills were provided to families and children through the project. Other community services and resources were also made available through the active liaison efforts of program personnel.

GOALS AND OBJECTIVES OF THE PROJECT

The major rationale on the home visitation component of the FDRP was predicated on the principle that parents are the primary teachers and sustaining caregiving figures in the infant's life. Affective bonds between parent and infant are extremely important for early learning. Thus it is imperative to support and strengthen parental abilities, potency, and pleasure in these functions. Specifically, the objective of maximizing family functioning was implemented by (a) contributing to parental knowledge about infant and child development and family nutrition, (b) modeling those skills which can foster parental enrichment of the infant's cognitive and social-emotional experiences, and (c) supporting the parent in her efforts to achieve a better life for herself.

Lally attributed the rationale for the work with parents to Saul Alinsky's theories of community organization. The goal of the parent program was to help families have "a say" in what is happening to them. The program was to support, rather than substitute for, parents. Work in the home focused on the parent rather than on the infant alone as an important figure in parent-infant transactions.

Four major theoretical contributions shaped the goals and objectives of the infant program. Piagetian theory suggested that the more varied and rich the opportunities for an infant's interactions with objects, people, and events in his environment, the greater were the chances that a child could accomplish successfully the developmental tasks of the sensorimotor and preoperational periods. The theory also suggested that caregivers needed to match environmental inputs to individual development levels carefully lest infants tune out environmental encounters as either too difficult or "old hat."

Language developmental theory suggested that adult modeling for and expanding of child language can promote increasing mastery of and pleasure in the uses of language. Contingent (i.e., dependent on a prior response) and appropriate responding to early language efforts should increase an infant's vocal repertoire. Appropriate adult labeling of people, objects, and events should increase the child's ability to decode words used by others.

Erikson's theory of developmental stages identified the growth of the basic trusting relationship between infant and caregiver as the primary emotional learning task of the first year of life. Emotional growth over the next few years would include increasing self-reliance and self-assurance concerning one's own needs and efforts as well as a sense of being able to take initiatives and to make more and more choices and decisions for oneself.

Together, Erikson's and Piaget's contributions provided the rationale for a curriculum in which "cognitive" and "social-emotional" development were wedded together conceptually. Further, not only can intellectual and affective development in the infant curriculum not be separated, but the curriculum itself cannot be viewed as "separate" from the living, loving, and learning environment of the infant. One goal of the program, therefore, was to devise ways to embed various aspects of the infant curriculum within the daily caregiving routines and activities carried out with babies.

The philosophies of Dewey and the British Infant Schools rounded-out the rationale for the toddler and preschooler program. Differentiated environments were arranged for the children so that they could choose activities freely within a program characterized and defined by spatial dimensions rather than by sequential time periods.

THE TEACHING-LEARNING FORMAT

The Children's Center program consisted of three main groupings which were designated to accommodate developmental stages.

The Infant Fold

Babies from six to fifteen months attended either a morning or an afternoon session. Four babies were assigned to each caregiver. Although tasks were cheerfully shared in the infant fold, each caregiver served as her infant's "special" person—for feeding, loving, comforting, "talking" together, and learning games. Cribs and feeding tables were available within the infant fold.

Caregivers arranged the environment to promote safe explorations; to encourage visual regard and coordination of seeing, reaching, and grasping; and to facilitate an infant's ability to provide learning experiences for himself or herself. Mobiles and stabiles were fastened to ceilings, walls, and cribs. Framed mirrors were placed at floor level where a crawling baby could come up and explore his own image visually. Mirrors were also attached to walls beside changing tables so that an infant who had just been diapered, washed, and combed could be propped to a sitting position to see him- or herself refreshed and happy.

Spatial aspects and arrangements were considered integral to good program planning. Open shelves with toys clearly visible and toy shelves with sliding doors were located near ground level. Small rug areas with low toy shelves, dressers, and bookshelves serving as boundaries from outside distractions permitted a caregiver to work with two or three babies at a time on a special activity.

The infant curriculum focused on ten aspects of development: (1) development of prehension skills—such as grasping and handling objects of different sizes and shapes; (2) development of the concept of object permanence—through peek-a-boo games and hide-a-toy activities with containers and cloths; (3) development of a means for achieving ends—such as pulling a string to get an attached toy, or bunching a chain to get it into a narrow-mouthed container; (4) development of new schemes in relation to objects—such as adorning oneself with a pop-it bead necklace or drinking from a cup; (5) development of a concept of causality which included the relation of actions to external results—such as turning a key to operate a mechanical toy; (6) development of a conception of objective space as continuous and within which all objects are contained and related; (7) de-

velopment of imitation and modeling skills—such as pat-a-cake; (8) development of language understanding and language communication, as well as
increasing enjoyment of stories and picture books; (9) development of
bodily and locomotion skills; (10) development of sense organs and an
increased repertoire of interpretable sensory experiences.

These developmental goals were translated by infant caregivers into
activities which could be carried out during the course of the day—for
example, at diapering time or when caregivers played with babies cozily on
the floor, or while they rocked a baby in a chair.

Positive reinforcement—by hugs, smiles, caresses, words, etc.—were
used to reward babies for trying new or slightly difficult tasks. Caregivers
were taught to end learning games on a happy note, rather than "pushing"
an infant to "perform." Games with multiple purposes were devised. For
example, a corridor of sorts was created within the large classroom by
placing three-foot-high divider screens along a line parallel to, but about
four feet from, the wall. Infants could enjoy a "run-run-run" game with
their energetic caregiver in this corridor. The caregiver sometimes popped
behind one of the screens and poked out her head at the side. Then she
called "peek-a-boo, Jimmy!" before ducking back behind the screen. The
infant, with peals of laughter, toddled to the screen and peered around to
find his teacher. She might have scooted to the opposite side of the screen
to play peek-a-boo from a new angle. The screen and corridor provided
opportunities for gestural imitation, large muscle play, object permanence
games, and for developing futher a joyous relationship between caregiver
and child.

The Transition Group

Babies from fifteen to eighteen months were in a special group, with full
day care five days a week, in which a more enriched and varied program of
activities was offered beyond the predominantly sensorimotor activities of
the infant fold. Here infants who only recently began to develop skills in
locomotion, self-feeding, coping with large spatial areas, and freedom of
choice, could develop the assurance, experience, and competence to deal
with the family-style world of the older toddler.

Family Style Education: Multi-age Differentiated-Environment Groupings

The program for eighteen- to sixty-month-old infants was somewhat akin
to the British Infant School in philosophy and structure. This program was
called "Family Style" since children of varying ages were together daily as
they typically would be in family settings. The children had freedom of

access to many classrooms during their full day's activities and freedom of choice in their selection of activities.

Two replicated modules of this family style structure exist. In each module, four major environmental areas were offered to the children. One or two teachers offered activities, help, and encouragement in each of the following areas:

A. *The large muscle area* Walkboards, large building blocks, cardboard boxes, slides, rocking boats, climbers, tumbling mats, and other such equipment encouraged the children to try activities involving large muscle and kinesthetic development. A housekeeping corner and dress-up corner invited children to carry out dramatic play and bodily expression. A table was set with mid-morning and post-nap snacks in this area. These snacks were freely available twice a day during an hour-long period of time which was well announced to the children.

B. *The small muscle area* Fine motor coordination was encouraged by an assortment of materials (for example: pegboards, puzzles, beads to string) which invited practice of prehension skills. Many of these toys were homemade at the Children's Center and often consisted of items (such as coffee cans plus clothespins and bottle caps to fill them) with which the toddler was already familiar at home.

C. *The sense experience area* In this area, materials and opportunities were provided for sensory experiences. Pasted in a cluster on a cardboard were bumpy kidney beans to touch. Stitched onto a burlap wall hanging was a puppy, whose body was made of plush fake-fur. Record players, and rhythm and music instruments were available here. A reading corner was provided with a comfortable couch and reachable shelves of attractive books. Taste sampling (for example, sweet honey; then sour lemon) and taste mixing (honey *on* lemon) were included in this area's ventures. Cinnamon, vanilla, and other scents could be smelled. Short movies were very popular. Intersensory activities of feeling enclosed containers for items to match others visible on the table were carried out here. Assorted gerbils, goldfish, and terraria offered further potential sensory explorations, always of course with the teacher's gentle assistance, both to furry creatures and to curious toddlers.

D. *The expressive area and snack area* Furniture groupings permitted several subdivisions of this major area which contained painting easels, tables for claywork and plastic arts, water-play tubs with many kinds of containers and sand, and sawdust or rice boxes with sifters and containers. Children's art creations were prominently displayed around the room.

The rules for use of each area were simple. Equipment must be left in the area where it was found. Toys may be used in creative ways but destructive behavior with toys or people is not permitted. Otherwise a child was free to spend as little or as much time in an area or with a given activity as he or she chose. The area rules were restated calmly and firmly whenever necessary. Agressive actions were followed immediately by the application of a "time out procedure" in a three-sided hallway cubby hole where the child's belongings were kept.

Many educators refer to educational arrangements similar to the one just described as "unstructured." We feel that the family style setting was very structured but that the structure was a spatial rather than a time-oriented one.

Additional areas were available in the program. The children could choose from a wide variety of wheeled toys and equipment which was available in a large gymnasium. Part of the gym served as a dormitory for toddlers at nap-time. There was an outdoor play area with both grassy and asphalted space. A large dining area comfortably accomodated the children who ate lunch family-style in groups with a teacher at each table. Gym, nap, and lunch occurred at scheduled times of the day.

Each curriculum area was used to implement as many program goals as possible. Thus, for example, the gym, outdoor play yard, and large muscle areas not only served to help toddlers develop muscles, body grace, game skills, and vigorous, coordinated body actions, but they also helped foster language enrichment and concept development. "Near" and "far" and "fast" and "slow" are polar adjectives whose concepts, for example, were easy to teach in connection with activities in large muscle areas.

Social skills were developed as children learned to play together with walkboards, slides, barrels, and other large play equipment. When two shiny new tricyles were introduced into the gymnasium, teachers made particular use of this occasion to enhance trust in adults and to teach "taking turns." When they promised a turn on a new trike to a toddler, teachers made sure to follow through on every promise, even when a toddler had run off to another part of the gym and forgotten. Teachers would go and find that toddler when his turn came. Because of the concern and efforts shown by their caregivers, the children increasingly learned to be patient and to wait for a turn as well as to share resources.

The large gym area also provided rich opportunities for socio-dramatic play. For example, a little girl rode up to an adult on her trike. "Fill 'er up!" she called out. "How many gallons of gas do you need me to pump?" asked the adult, entering into her service-station job with gusto. "Two," answered the child. "There you are—two gallons of gas," replied the adult while vigorously pantomiming. The child pretended to pay for the gas, the adult thanked her, and off went the trike-alias-automobile. The housekeeping corner, of course, lent itself especially well to spontaneous role-playing episodes. But teachers who were quick at picking up child cues encouraged dramatic play and increased its range and complexity in all of the open-education areas provided by the program.

Although the open-education program promoted early self-actualization and independence, children were encouraged in all areas to use adults as resource people and to turn to adults when in difficulty rather than to use physical threats or force. When some children were exploring, on their own, new ways of using heaps of red play dough which had been set out on a table along with tooth-picks and plastic cups in the expressive area, one child "hoarded" a good portion of the play area. The other child said something, but his objections were ignored. Then he turned, searched the room for the teacher, and called out, "Hey, Mrs. Khan, Jackie is not sharing with me." The teacher moved to the table quietly and restated sharing rules in a helpful and positive manner. Another episode involved a child who grew so angry while at play in one area with her friend that she marched out of that area and down the hallway into another area. Before she left she explained to the teacher stationed in the first area, "I've got to get out of here for a while and cool down 'cause Jenny is making me so mad." By allowing free choice of movement into activities, the open education model seemed to facilitate the learning of social skills such as choosing nonaggressive action alternatives in frustrating situations.

Teachers noticed that the more alternative activities they provided in a given area, the fewer were the frictions likely to develop among little children. This does not mean that elaborate setups or equipment were necessary. A tub of sawdust with plastic toy animals hidden within the tub made a surprisingly feelable experience. One ingenious teacher created a Rube Goldberg kind of game with a large metal wash basin into which he fed a long tube made of pipes fitted together. Each child asked the teacher who was stationed near this novel game for between one and four marbles to shoot (during his or her turn) down through the tube and into the basin. The teacher had an old coffee pot in which to collect the marbles. From this pot he scooped up the marbles and placed them one by one in a child's palm while both he and the child elaborately counted aloud the number of marbles which the child had requested. Depending on how the child shot it through the tube, the marble made gentle or wild gyrations in the basin. Fascinated, some children stayed as long as half an hour at this activity. Thus, open education does not mean the child must always structure every encounter with the environment by himself or herself entirely. Teachers created and arranged activities. Sometimes they themselves structured an activity which was then made available among the choices offered to the children in the family-style groups. The principal, for instance, brought in wheat which the children helped her to grind, make into dough, and later bake for a special afternoon snack. Reading of stories was frequently initiated by a child's request, or by a teacher's invitation.

As the infants grew toward school age, a twenty-minute, highly structured activity was offered two or three times a week. Pairs of children, carefully chosen to ensure that temperaments and abilities were compatible, were taken from the open-education areas to a special, rather bare room where carefully and minutely sequenced learning activities involving classifications (by color, shape, number, etc.), seriations, and sensory discrimination learning experiences were presented. The Children's Center principal and teachers spent months with a jig-saw, sanding paper, and lacquer paints creating these materials in accordance with suggestions from the Sprigle program in Florida. Each child in the tutorial setting had a set of materials to use during the session. This special tutorial situation was designed to extend language use and to develop cognitive understanding through the child's involvement with the materials. Perhaps even more important is that these small group sessions enhanced a child's self-esteem through successful experiences and positive social interactions with the partner and the teaching adult. Frequently, for example, after a child finished taking a turn in which he may have successfully guessed that the wooden shape he was feeling in a paper bag was a heart and not a diamond, he would himself place shapes in the bag and ask the teacher to close her eyes and take her turn at guessing.

For handicapped infants and toddlers, this combination of an open education model for infants and toddlers enhanced by highly structured and sequenced small group or tutorial sessions may be potentially highly valuable. Particular kinds of tutorial therapeutic work may well be indicated for particular kinds of disabilities in order to minimize them. However, the advantage of the open-education model is that, in addition to highly structured activities which may be therapeutically necessary, the young child gets a chance to direct his or her own experiences within a variety of areas. This opportunity for choice and for breadth of experience can enhance the self-concept of a child whose options are often doubly restricted by a physical handicap and by social and institutional constraints.

In accordance with the program objectives of embedding curricula within caregiving situations, teachers did a great deal of modeling and praising during the course of early routines. For example, "I like the way you walked up those stairs holding on so carefully," remarked Miss K. to a toddler as he climbed one of the long stairways in the center. Mealtime was a great time for sociable talk, for learning eating and cleaning-up routines, and for making choices from among the family-style serving bowls of food. The children were offered many different kinds of vegetables and other foods as well as foods with which they were familiar in their own families. They responded positively, both to the variety of foods and toward the mealtime situation in general. Nap or rest time on cots followed the midday meal. An adult was available at all times in each nap area. As children gradually woke from naps, they were able to use first one and then another of the program areas. The children became accustomed to the "need to wait" until the clock showed 2:30, or until a sufficient number of personnel were available after lunch to staff the areas.

Outdoor play was encouraged daily if weather permitted. Syracuse's generous annual supply of snow added a special dimension to the "environmental encounters" available to toddlers. Field trips were frequently held. One of the center's bus drivers was particularly proud of his work on developing field trips for the children. Along with suggested sites, he listed the different kinds of Piagetian developmental experiences he thought each field trip site would make possible.

Guests were invited to visit the center. One guest brought in an especially fancy guinea pig. Another guest played the cello for the children. There was a kind of ease and genuine social responsiveness and interest among the children toward the strangers who visited them.

The small, bright yellow center buses began departing for homes at approximately 4:00 in the afternoon. The buses were equipped with seats and safety belts for all the children. Each had an adult rider as well as a driver. Often, bus routes were complicated because a parent telephoned to say that she could not be at home and that the child should be left, for example, at grandmother's house.

NATURE OF PARENT INVOLVEMENT

For the home visitation component of the present program, a deliberate choice was made to select child development trainers (CDTs) who were indigenous to the low-income community they were to serve. (Dr. Ira Gordon in Florida has already highlighted the special strengths which paraprofessionals could contribute to a home visitation project.)

The CDTs began their visits in the home during the last three months of the mother's pregnancy. The longer a CDT worked with a family, the more her role expanded to become more directly relevant to the needs and concerns of that particular family. Problems in center families often involved severe emotional, legal, economic, and health stresses. Such problems constantly required the CDT to ask for further training and knowledge. CDTs always took family nutrition and infant development information to the homes. They always demonstrated learning games and modeled varieties of positive teaching styles for the mothers. Additionally, as the need arose, CDTs took on a wide spectrum of jobs. These included: teaching artificial respiration; disseminating sex education information; sharing housekeeping tips; suggesting alternative ways to discipline children; making referrals to legal, medical, and social services through key contact people in agencies; and carrying out a recipe for making a casserole dinner with a mother.

CDTs made toy and book lending kits available to the mothers. Both CDTs and mothers constantly created new games and activities to promote learning. The home visitors took mothers shopping, to the library, and to the zoo. They organized parent group meetings on topics requested by parents, and assumed active leadership roles in Friday morning workshops at the Children's Center. At these workshops, mothers carried out projects such as sewing clothes, making cardboard furniture, and using styrofoam egg cartons to create infant crib stabiles and colorful wastebaskets.

The CDTs served an important liaison function between the home and the Center. They eased possible misunderstandings over a misplaced mitten. They alerted teachers to critical home situations (such as the death of a beloved grandfather or the distress caused when a child witnessed an abusive boyfriend becoming violent with a mother). These situations may have been related to changes in a child's sociableness or his responsiveness to learning, and they required special sensitivity and support for the child from the center staff.

Later, the home visitors helped the mothers to become the children's advocates with respect to the public school system. CDTs arranged meetings of groups of mothers in order to talk about the importance of the family's ongoing role in the child's learning career as he or she enters the school system.

The positive concern of the CDT for the families she served was fundamental to the success of program efforts. One way this concern was shown was by accommodating weekly visits to the mother's work or school schedule, even when this meant evening, weekend, or very early morning visits. The home visitors were available by telephone at any hour. Mothers stated that they regarded the CDTs as trusted friends rather than just people with a job to be done. Many remarked that they would not have paid much attention to the educational needs of the infants had they not known the home visitor.

Weekly observations of the home visitor formed a continuous record of how and how much a family was involved with its baby's development. Parental involvement, when positive and continued, was expected to sustain the infant's development long after outside intervention ceased.

STAFF DEVELOPMENT

Both pre-service and in-service staff training were integrated into the Children's Center program. Early each autumn, the Center was closed for an intensive two-week training period. All personnel, including the kitchen staff, a pediatrician, bus drivers, a bookkeeper, and secretaries, participated in these sessions. Emphasis was placed less on long lectures than on workshops, role playing, and small-group talks and demonstrations. Often teachers or CDTs with special skills in an area such as "songs and rhythm games" or "making books for babies" would lead one of these sessions. Research staff with expertise in topics such as nutrition, Piagetian games, language development, or handling discipline problems, conducted other sessions. Frequent use was made of infant growth and infant care films such as "Learning to Learn in Infancy" by Dr. Joseph Stone and "How Babies Learn" by Dr. Bettye Caldwell.

A training handbook was used in the sessions to give explicit attention to the subject areas, materials, and techniques in which infant caregivers must be trained. Topics included in the book were developing a healthy personality, nutrition and diet, large muscle skills, pick-up and handling skills, sense experiences, Piagetian development, infant language and pre-reading skills, use of living spaces, toy-making for babies, and use of community resources.

During the intensive annual preservice training period, we found it very helpful to provide trainees with blank diaries in which to record their experiences. Their records and comments about what they learned, their criticisms and puzzlements, and summaries of the material presented, helped us to provide better training. These diaries ultimately served as a personal resource and refresher book for the caregiver on the job.

In-service training, carried on almost daily during children's nap times, took a variety of forms. The principal of the Children's Center was responsible for many aspects of training—particularly those concerned with the safety, comfort, and well-being of the children. Other teacher-trainers were responsible for in-classroom work with teachers. The teacher-trainers modeled such skills as how to handle behavior problems, how to use on-the-spot situations to help a child to explore and learn more independently, and how to facilitate pleasurable social interactions among children.

In-service training was supplemented by regular, written feedback to teachers from testing personnel. The feedback summarized each child's interests, competencies, and difficulties in relating to test materials, activities, and the interpersonal milieu of the assessment situation. When necessary, case conferences were held which drew upon the tester, teacher, home visitor, and pediatrician's knowledge of a child who might have been having problems that required special attention.

Sensitivity to the periodic needs of caregivers to resharpen their skills and rededicate themselves to the program objectives was important. Some staff meetings were therefore devoted to specific topics of concern, for the sake of smoother center functioning, and to program policy considerations. Teachers also met to create learning materials and to share ideas for facilitating child development in areas where difficulties were encountered. One teacher, having noticed that a commercial lacing shoe was too difficult for his toddlers, screwed four eye-screws at the corners of a plywood square. Toddlers found they could successfully practice pulling a shoe lace through the large holes in the square pattern.

Administrative Considerations

The facility in which the FDRP was housed was a large church building. Thus a great many rooms were available which could serve as activity spaces for the four major areas of each family style module, for the infant fold, for the home visitors. A large kitchen, a dining hall, a gymnasium, an outdoor play yard, a visitor's lounge, offices, testing rooms, and spacious hallways were also available.

The spatial areas required by the family style program may be larger than that available to some programs. We have been involved in transmitting our program philosophy and materials to the staff in a Kentucky program, however, and can report that they have satisfactorily "miniaturized" some of the areas by placing activity areas in different parts of a single room when necessitated by space restrictions.

The cost of the FDRP per child per week was eighty dollars. This included all payments for the research staff, transportation staff, bus leasing, kitchen staff, computer time, substitute teachers, bus drivers and riders, a computer analyst, a bookkeeper, a receptionist, food purchases, diaper service, teachers, home visitors, and supervisors. This cost included a travel budget for all home visitors and research personnel who gathered data in homes. Additionally, the figure covered the cost of a staff person to handle about 1,000 visitors per year and the dissemination of free center reports and publications. The cost of equipment included toy purchases, art supplies, tables, chairs, cots, cribs, feeding tables, large-muscle toys such as slides, swings, etc. This cost averaged about $700 per year. Initially, of course, investments for infant furnishings were higher.

The home visitors had their own supervisor. The kitchen staff had an expert nutritionist as their supervisor. Teacher-trainers from the research staff and from the master-teachers at the center supervised teacher-training during in-service work. Some staff members served multiple jobs; our bookkeeper, for example, was also a fine tester of toddlers. The recruiters, who rang doorbells to find project and matching control group families, were also responsible for bringing children in for assessments. The program director also had multiple jobs; for example—creating learning games and teaching them to teacher trainers, training testers, creating and searching for appropriate assessment instruments, helping find new materials and activities that home visitors could use with mothers, and writing reports.

The principal's job was also very flexibly conceived. She might one afternoon be holding a discussion about the dangers of some foods—like peanuts—for babies. Another day she might be diapering a toddler because a staff member was ill.

In general, a great deal of decision-making was required of the staff in implementing their roles. Teachers assigned themselves on rotating weeks to different family-style areas. Infant-fold caregivers were remarkable about sharing responsibilities for babies when one or another caregiver went on a coffee break. One ingenious infant-fold teacher softly played tambourine rhythms to which babies could bounce during a 10 minute time period when the co-caregiver was called out for a phone call!

PROGRAM EVALUATION

Evaluation measures were chosen or created for each area of interest and each phase of the program. Included were measures of how the children were faring developmentally, measures of parent and family and of home visitor and center program effectiveness from the parents' point of view.

Evaluation measures were both formative and summative, that is, in many cases, evaluation was used to help teachers and home visitors understand a child's strengths and difficulties better so that more relevant experiences could be devised for a particular child.

Two different longitudinal control groups of children three years or older were formed. One was a control group of low-income, low-education infants who had not been in an intervention program. These infants were carefully matched with center children for the following at-birth variables: sex, ethnicity, parity, maternal age, and marital status. Another contrast group consisted of children (matched for age and sex) who came from intact families of college-educated parents. All children were tested under "optimal" conditions; that is, children were made very comfortable, fed meals when necessary, and returned, when necessary, for extra sessions to complete tests.

Infant and Child Assessments

Developmental achievements. The Cattell Infant Intelligence Scale was used with infants under twenty-four months and the Stanford Binet Scale with older children. At thirty-six and forty-eight months of age, the mean IQ of center children was about ten points higher than their low-income controls, whose mean scores were well within the normal IQ range. High-education contrast group children, however, scored more than twenty points above center children's scores. As the infants grew toward school age, other cognitive assessments such as the Boehm Test of Basic Concepts and the Caldwell Preschool Inventory were added to the library.

Language measures. Research has shown that measures of language functions in infancy can be better predictors of later intellective performance than standard developmental tests. With infants from five to thirty months, the "Early Language Assessment Scale" (ELAS) was used to assess infant ability (1) to understand the meanings of words, gestures, and items (such as food, furniture, and toys), and (2) to label with appropriate vocalizations and words (and to communicate about) objects, people, animals, and events. An observational measure, "Classroom Language Observation Checklist" (CLOC) was created to observe and note the different ways in which language was expressed and used by two- and three-year-old children in natural classroom interactions. Selected subtests of the "Illinois Test of Psycholinguistic Abilities" (ITPA) were administered to children from forty-eight months onward. At forty-eight months, center children score significantly higher than their low-income controls on four out of seven ITPA subtests administered.

Piagetian measures. A prominent curricular component of the infant-fold involved presenting sensorimotor tasks and arranging the environment so that infants could acquire sensorimotor skills through their own explorations. The assessment battery at six, twelve, and eighteen months included a variety of Piagetian scales to assess: comprehension of means-ends relations, causality, and spatial relations; ability to perform general gestural and vocal imitations; and development of a variety of schemas to use with objects. Center infants at twelve months tended to do better than control infants on difficult object permanence tasks. Teachers also kept daily wall chart records of the Piagetian experiences and games which they presented to babies.

Social-emotional assessments. Positive social-emotional functioning in infancy is seen as the foundation for the growth of early learning. The Cornell Descriptive Scanning Record of Infant Activity, developed by Dr. Henry Ricciuti, was utilized to compare center infants with Cornell University nursery infants from intact middle-class homes. Center infants observed from six to thirteen months seemed to be more alert, talkative, and physically active than Cornell infants. They smiled, vocalized, and engaged in playful interactions more frequently than the group of babies from optimal home environments. These data are reassuring in the light of oft expressed fears that group care of infants may depress their social-emotional functioning.

The "Bayley Infant Behavior Record" was used in conjunction with each developmental assessment. The data collected by using the "Record" reflected the infant's responses to easy and difficult tasks in a test situation and to test personnel.

Emmerich's "Observation Scales of Personal Social Constructs" were used with children aged thirty-six months and onward within the center's environments to assess children's relations and encounters with each other, with adults, and with tasks. Ratings by teachers on Coopersmith's "Rating Form," on Beller's "Autonomous Achievement Striving Scale," and on Schaefer's "Classroom Behavior Inventory" and "Classroom Behavior Checklist" provided additional social-emotional measures.

Medical measures. Lead poisoning and iron-deficiency-anemia tests as well as dental, visual, and hearing examinations were arranged by the pediatrician associated with the center.

Family measures. The home visitors supplied weekly and monthly ratings of the mother-infant and mother-CDT relations they observed in the homes. They also obtained baby diet information and diet information on expectant mothers. The "Family Data Record" (FDR) was used to gather demographic information.

Three major interviews which reflected family functioning were administered in the home. One was Caldwell's "Inventory of Home Stimulation" (STIM). STIM consisted of an interview plus observation checklist administered in the home while the child was awake and could be observed in interaction with his mother. STIM was available in two forms, for families with younger and older preschoolers, and was based on the assumption of eight areas or factors in the home which were presumptive for encouraging early development. Another was the "Implicit Parental Learning Theory" (IPLET) interview, which attempted to discover the variety of methods that mothers used in handling ordinary developmental infant and child behaviors. The third was the "Parent Evaluation of Program and Prognosis for Educational Responsibility" (PEPPER), an instrument designed to help parents verbalize their feelings about the program and how they perceived the role of the home visitor.

When children were five years of age, all program and low-income control mothers were videotaped in a teaching situation with their children as well as in an episode where they made up a story about a picture for the child. In the teaching interaction, the mother was asked to make a triangle by using the Etch-A-Sketch toy with her child. Maternal teaching strategies were coded by global, bi-polar, social-emotional scale ratings as well as by the APPROACH interaction coding system developed by Caldwell and Honig.

Teacher measures. Program outcomes were tied directly to the degree to which program goals were implemented and to the quality of the implementation. We developed a series of easy-to-use and reliable checklists, called "Assessing the Behaviors of Caregivers" (ABC) for monitoring in-classroom teacher behavior. ABC-I was for teachers of infants under fifteen months; ABC-II was for toddlers' teachers; and ABC-III was for teachers of preschoolers who were three to five years old. Behavior frequency profiles of "master" teachers, i.e., teachers with many years of experience and training in the Children's Center, were used as guidelines in individual training programs to improve teacher skills, such as skills in eliciting infant vocalizations or arranging Piagetian spatial concepts activities for babies, in specific areas.

Measures we wish we had taken. Although teachers encouraged children to use each of the available open environmental areas freely, no data are available which could relate the actual frequency of the children's participation in each of the four areas over a period of time to their developmental scores and change scores. Perhaps this is not so critical a point if one considers that implementation of program goals in all areas was vigorously pursued. Nevertheless, the data would have been of theoretical interest in illuminating issues of concern, for example, between those who are proponents of more structured curricular equipment, such as puzzles, and those who recommend more process-oriented toys, such as block play. Unfortunately funds were not available for the large amount of observation time (in each area with each child) which this kind of measurement would have required.

FUTURE PLANS

The termination of funding resources for 1976 made future planning for the center a rather tenuous exercise. Center personnel, however, were both extensively and intensively skilled in the art of caregiving, both with infants and preschoolers, as well as in the art of working harmoniously together as a team. One possible hope would be to get board of education support for establishing infant nurseries in local high schools so that infants and toddlers of staff, faculty, and pregnant teenage students could use the facility. Present center caregivers could staff these nurseries full-time. They could serve as excellent "caregiving" role-models for teenage parents and for high school students in human development courses.

Dr. Lally has submitted grant proposals asking for funds to continue observations, assessments, and interviews with the families and children who have been served to date in this project. Since the test of home intervention efforts lies in family support for the child's development *after* intervention ceases, such support seems crucial in assessing the long-term effectiveness of the omnibus model.

"If wishes were king," we should of course very much want to see the philosophy and curriculum implementation of the infant-fold and family-style differentiated-classroom-areas widely disseminated and also replicated in our community, perhaps in a "rainbow mix" model which would include babies from differing socioeconomic and ethnic groups. There was a joyous self-confidence, sociability, and language facility exhibited by the four-year-olds who grew since infancy in the world of the Children's Center. Their behavior increased our belief in a program model which translated Eriksonian social-emotional principles and Piagetian cognitive-developmental principles into inseparable and essential ingredients of nursery staff and parenting practices. Within the Children's Center, implementation of such a model provided a nourishing milieu in which infants flourished.

BIBLIOGRAPHY

Caldwell, B. M., and Richmond, J. B. The Children's Center in Syracuse, New York. In L. L. Dittmann (Ed.), *Early child care: The new perspectives.* New York: Atherton Press, 1968.

Gordon, I. J., and Lally, J. R. *Intellectual stimulation for infants and toddlers.* Gainesville, Florida: Institute for Development of Human Resources, University of Florida, 1967.

Honig, A. S. Curriculum for infants in day care. *Child Welfare,* 1974, 53 (10), 663-642.

Honig, A. S., and Lally, J. R. *Infant caregiving: A design for training.* New York: Media Projects, Inc., 1972.

Lally, J. R., and Honig, A. S. Education of infants and toddlers from low-income and low-education backgrounds: Support for the family's role and identify. In B. Friedlander, G. Kirk, & G. Steritt (Eds.), *Infant assessment and intervention.* New York: Brunner/Mazel, 1975.

Lally, J. R., and Honig, A. S. The Family Development Research Program. In R. Parker (Ed.), *The preschool in action.* New York: Allyn & Bacon, 1975. (in press)

Lally, J. R., Honig, A. S., and Caldwell, B. M. Training paraprofessionals for work with infants and toddlers. *Young Children,* 1973, 28 (3), 173-182.

CHAPTER 7

An Introduction to the Carolina Abecedarian Project

Craig T. Ramey,
Margaret C. Holmberg,
Joseph H. Sparling,
and Albert M. Collier

HISTORY AND DESCRIPTION OF PRESENT PROGRAM

Researchers have known for many years that children from low socio-economic backgrounds tend disproportionately to fall victim to develop-mental retardation. Although some of the retardation can be traced to organic causes, most developmentally retarded children have no identifi-able organic damage. It is, therefore, likely that some set of environmental influences or experiences accounts for the needless stunting of potential among seriously disadvantaged children.

The Carolina Abecedarian Project, a component of the Frank Porter

ALBERT M. COLLIER is an Assistant Professor of Pediatrics at the University of North Carolina School of Medicine and the Medical Director at the Frank Porter Graham Child Development Center. His major professional interest is in the effects of infectious respiratory diseases and their complications on child development.

MARGARET COOPER HOLMBERG is the Director of the Early Childhood Education Program at the Frank Porter Graham Child Development Center. Her major professional interests include early childhood and day care programs, the training of teachers who work with young children, and the development of social behaviors in young children.

CRAIG T. RAMEY is Assistant Director for Research at the Frank Porter Graham Center. His interests are primarily in the area of learning and social de-velopment in infancy and early childhood.

JOSEPH J. SPARLING is an Investigator working with the infant curriculum at the Frank Porter Graham Center. His major professional interests are child de-velopment and curriculum development.

Graham Child Development Center (FPG), was begun in 1972 to investigate issues in sociocultural developmental retardation. Basically the project seeks to accomplish four major objectives:

1. To demonstrate that sociocultural retardation can be prevented through child-centered early education

2. To develop and evaluate an infant curriculum that can be used in a variety of educational settings

3. To discover which psychological and biological processes and mechanisms are affected by early intervention

4. To describe the relationships among psychological, biological and family attributes during the first five years of the child's life

Selection of Subjects

North Carolina Memorial Hospital, the University of North Carolina's teaching hospital, is the primary referral source for potential subjects for the project. Through its various prenatal clinics pass most of the expectant mothers in Orange County who are likely to meet the criteria for inclusion in our sample.

Once a family is identified as being potentially eligible, the supervisor of the project's infant nursery contacts that family. The supervisor arranges to see them at their home for an interview to explain the project and to determine whether they are interested in participating. During this interview, the supervisor informs the parents that the Frank Porter Graham Center is conducting a long-term study on how children from economically limited families grow and develop during infancy and early childhood and that the program goal is to find out what things make a baby healthy and competent. The supervisor explains that the study consists of two separate programs. The first program (the control group) involves periodic assessment of the child and other family members, especially the mother. The second program (the experimental group) involves the day care services which will be detailed later in this chapter. It is explained that all mothers will be paid for the time that they spend in any of the assessment sessions, either at the FPG Center or in their homes. Further, all transportation to and from the center is provided for the experimental group daily and for both groups whenever parents cannot transport themselves to scheduled assessments. The supervisor also informs the families that they will be assigned to one program or the other after the baby is born and its sex is

TABLE 1

HIGH RISK INDEX

MOTHER'S EDUCATIONAL LEVEL (LAST GRADE COMPLETED)	WEIGHTS	FATHER'S EDUCATIONAL LEVEL (LAST GRADE COMPLETED)	WEIGHTS	FAMILY INCOME	WEIGHTS
6	8	6	8	1,000	8
7	7	7	7	1,001-2,000	7
8	6	8	6	2,001-3,000	6
9	3	9	3	3,001-4,000	5
10	2	10	2	4,001-5,000	4
11	1	11	1	5,001-6,000	0
12	0	12	0		

OTHER INDICATIONS OF HIGH RISK AND POINT VALUES

PTS.	
3	1. FATHER IS ABSENT FOR REASONS OTHER THAN HEALTH OR DEATH.
3	2. MATERNAL RELATIVES ARE ABSENT IN LOCAL AREA (I.E., PARENTS, GRANDPARENTS, OR BROTHERS OR SISTERS OF MAJORITY AGE).
3	3. SIBLINGS OF SCHOOL AGE WHO ARE ONE OR MORE GRADES BEHIND AGE-APPROPRIATE GRADE OR WHO SCORE EQUIVALENTLY LOW ON SCHOOL ADMINISTERED ACHIEVEMENT TESTS ARE PRESENT.
3	4. PAYMENTS HAVE BEEN RECEIVED FROM WELFARE AGENCIES WITHIN PAST THREE YEARS.
3	5. RECORD OF FATHER'S WORK INDICATES UNSTABLE AND UNSKILLED OR SEMI-SKILLED LABOR.
3	6. RECORDS OF MOTHER'S OR FATHER'S IQS SHOW SCORES OF 90 OR BELOW.
3	7. RECORDS OF SIBLING'S IQS SHOW SCORES OF 90 OR BELOW.
3	8. RELEVANT SOCIAL AGENCIES IN THE COMMUNITY INDICATE THAT THE FAMILY IS IN NEED OF ASSISTANCE.
1	9. ONE OR MORE MEMBERS OF THE FAMILY HAS SOUGHT COUNSELING OR PROFESSIONAL HELP IN THE PAST THREE YEARS.
1	10. OTHER SPECIAL CIRCUMSTANCES, NOT INCLUDED IN ANY OF THE ABOVE, ARE LIKELY CONTRIBUTORS TO CULTURAL OR SOCIAL DISADVANTAGE.

CRITERION FOR INCLUSION IN HIGH RISK SAMPLE IS A SCORE ≥ 11.

determined.

If the supervisor determines that the family potentially meets the criteria for inclusion in the program, the expectant mother is invited to the center for a series of interviews. These interviews are designed to assess her attitudes toward child-rearing practices, to gather detailed family background information, and to assess the mother's IQ.

One purpose of these interviews is to rate the family on an experimental "High-Risk Index" which is shown in Table 1. Weights are assigned to the various factors on the basis of our "best guess" of their relative importance. Because there is little epidemiological data concerning the factors linked to developmental retardation, it is impossible to assign empirically-derived weights to each factor. It is hoped, however, that as the sample families are followed, it will be possible to derive empirical weights through multiple regression analyses.

After target children are born, qualifying families are pair-matched on sex of the child, maternal IQ, number of siblings, and total high-risk scores; the members of each pair are randomly assigned to either the experimental or the control group. Table 2 contains a summary of the demographic and psychological characteristics of the first two cohorts of children that were admitted to the program. To date, fifty-nine families have been offered membership in either the experimental or control groups and fifty-eight have accepted. All families, except for three whose infants died in the first year of life, have remained in the program. One child who died was diagnosed as a "crib-death," and the other children died from heart failure. One child was in the experimental group, and two children were in the control group.

Components of the Program

Both the experimental and the control subjects receive the following services:

1. *Family support through social services* On the basis of parental requests and routine staff visits to families, the Abecedarian Project seeks to provide all families with goods, services, or guidance (in such areas as legal aid, family planning, food, clothing, or housing) that will help keep the families intact.

2. *Nutritional supplements* All children in the experimental group receive the bulk of their nutrition at the day care center. Breakfast, lunch, and an afternoon snack are served each day. As a control for nutritional differences between the experimental and control groups, the control group receives an unlimited supply of free formula for as long as needed.

3. *Transportation* Transportation to and from the center is provided for all subjects participating in the project.

4. *Payment for participation* All mothers are paid for participating in any non-medical evaluations.

TABLE 2

SELECTED DEMOGRAPHIC CHARACTERISTICS OF THE
FIRST TWO YEARLY COHORTS ADMITTED
TO THE ABECEDARIAN PROGRAM

GROUP	MEAN MATER-NAL IQ	MEAN FAMILY INCOME	MEAN MATER-NAL EDUCA-TION	MEAN HIGH RISK SCORE	MEAN MATER-NAL AGE	MEAN NUM-BER OF SIB-LINGS
GROUP 1 CENTER (10 FEMALES, 4 MALES)	80.0	$1,964.28	10.14	19.78	19.7	.7
GROUP 1 HOME (10 FEMALES, 4 MALES)	78.14	$1,428.57	10.43	21.2	23.93	1.6
GROUP 2 CENTER (7 FEMALES, 8 MALES)	85.78	$ 642.86	10.35	18.93	17.64	.14
GROUP 2 HOME (8 FEMALES, 6 MALES)	85.57	$ 928.57	10.21	20.78	18.07	.36

5. *Diaper service* Disposable diapers are provided free to the control subjects as an inducement for continuing to participate and as a potentially beneficial health measure.

6. *Medical care* The goals of the medical component are to provide complete medical care and to study respiratory tract infections and complications in children comprising the FPG longitudinal population. The children are permitted to attend sessions at the center, except with chickenpox and measles, when ill.

Medical care at FPG is provided by a health care team consisting of a pediatrician, a family nurse practitioner, a pediatric nurse practitioner, and a licensed practical nurse. The offices of each member of the health care team, along with two examining rooms and facilities for simple laboratory tests, are located in the center. Primary pediatric care at the FPG Center is given by the family nurse practitioner and the pediatric nurse practitioner, both under the supervision of the pediatrician. This care includes regularly scheduled well child assessments, administration of appropriate immunizations, counseling of families, and initial assessment of all illnesses.
Well child care. Well child assessments are made at ages two, four, six, nine,

twelve, eighteen, and twenty-four months and yearly thereafter. During assessments, parents are present for an exchange of information and counseling. The assessment includes obtaining a health and social history, administering a complete physical examination, and counseling and teaching parents in such areas as feeding and nutrition, cleanliness, skin care, elimination, accident prevention, child growth, development and behavior, weaning, toilet training, parent-child-sibling interactions, and dental hygiene. Parents are encouraged to express their concerns and discuss problems.

During assessments, appropriate immunizations, as recommended by the American Academy of Pediatrics, are given. A skin test for tuberculosis is given yearly; a sickle cell prep is obtained at the age of nine to twelve months from all black children; and a hematocrit is done at age nine and eighteen months and yearly thereafter. Routine screening for vision and hearing is also provided annually.

If abnormalities are found, either during the physical exam or later in the laboratory work, the pediatrician at the center consults with special clinics in the North Carolina Memorial Hospital; referrals are made when necessary. In providing comprehensive health care for the children at FPG, the nurse practitioners and the pediatrician work with other social agencies in the community to coordinate various services needed by children and their families. The health care team also cooperates with other disciplines within the center on various aspects of the program involving health data and the needs of specific children.

Ill child care. In addition to providing well child care, the nurse practitioner is responsible for the initial assessment of all illnesses seen in the center. There is daily surveillance of all children for signs of illness. If possibility of illness is suspected, the nurse practitioner first obtains as much history as possible from the child care staff and parents. She then does the physical examination, performs appropriate laboratory tests, and makes a decision about the nature of the illness. In cases of mild illness, the nurse practitioner manages treatment on the basis of pre-established standing orders. With more severe illness, a physician's consultation is obtained. Parents are informed of the nature of the child's ailment, and the prescribed treatment is discussed with the parent by phone or through a visit to the home. Treatment is checked during and at the end of the illness as a follow-up measure. Care for control children is provided by the Primary Care Clinic at North Carolina Memorial Hospital.

THEORETICAL RATIONALE FOR THE PROJECT

The Abecdarian Project does not assume that sensory deprivation is the major cause of the developmental retardation experienced by high risk children. (If this were our assumption, a program of global, general stimulation might seem appropriate.) We assume instead that the problem is, more nearly, that the high risk child receives vague or competing sensory messages which he cannot use at the moment he receives them. This assumption leads us to define our curriculum development task as: (1) designing an organized resource bank of unambiguous experiences or activities, and (2) making each activity available to the child at a time and in such a way that he can use and master it successfully.

The educational experiences or activities of the Abecedarian Project are collectively called the "Carolina Infant Curriculum." The system through which this curriculum establishes its goals has its origins in the theoretical position presented by Ralph Tyler in 1950 and later elaborated upon by others. Within Tyler's framework, curriculum objectives are seen as the product of a number of interacting sources or factors. (These factors are the learner, the society, and the subject matter—according to Tyler's original formulation.) The present formulation is an expansion and restatement of the interacting sources which now include: (1) parent value judgements, (2) developmental theory (from Piaget), (3) developmental facts, and (4) professional value judgements. Although developmental facts and Piagetian theory are two of the interacting sources which are used in defining curriculum goals, it is inaccurate to say that a major objective of the curriculum is to accelerate developmental milestones or to hasten the acquisition of concepts, such as object permanence. The Carolina Infant Curriculum is better summarized through some of its professional value judgement statements, such as "Each child should progressively gain an expectation of success, a sense of control, and a style of task orientation." By viewing these broad statements through the structure of Piagetian theory and by using the detail offered by developmental facts and parent value judgements (e.g., "I want my twelve month old to drink from a cup."), specific curriculum objectives are generated. Information from each of the four source areas is identified as material for each new curriculum objective. By uniting, thoughtfully, four diverse bits of information, a single curriculum is created.

The Curriculum

The Carolina Infant Curriculum (i.e., the content of the educational program) is designed as a series of games or activities called "curriculum items." Each item is described in a one-page, teacher/parent guide sheet, that is written in simple language and has photographs to illustrate important points. Over 300 curriculum items have been developed. These relate to language, motor, social, and cognitive development, and together are thought of as a "curriculum resource bank."

Much of the teaching and learning at all ages occurs in a one-to-one interaction between adult and child. As children progress in age, the curriculum items are increasingly incorporated into the "classroom centers" in which small groups of children interact with each other and the adult teacher. At all ages, each child has an individual prescription of curriculum items. These prescriptions are revised every three weeks and contain from two to six items for each child. While these prescriptions are in effect, teachers creatively and consciously make sure that each child has frequent exposure to the curriculum items of his prescription.

Any curriculum that depends upon periodic prescriptions must include tools to help the teachers regularly observe each child's status. The Carolina Infant Curriculum provides a developmental chart to assist the teacher in maintaining a broad perspective on development. Available for each of the first three years of life is a checklist of developmental facts on which the teacher may record the status of the individual child. Once the teacher determines, through observation, the status of a child in a particular area (such as language), he or she searches the curriculum resource bank for a match between child status and one or more curriculum items. In the Abecedarian Project, a curriculum developer takes major responsibility for this observe/search/match process. Clearly, this will be a teacher or parent function when the curriculum is disseminated for use in other settings.

The adult teacher and the child interact by using the prescribed items as a natural and integral part of their daily lives for a period of three weeks. Then, on the basis of the adult's observations, new items are introduced or old ones are continued. Since this procedure is individualized, it is useful to document the variety and quantity of each child's actual curriculum experiences. In the Abecedarian Project, this documentation is accomplished through a cumulative record of all prescriptions and a record of daily tallies which shows the number of times an activity has been carried out.

Are the ideas and activities suggested in the Carolina Infant Curriculum new? Very few of them are. We have tried to collect many of the good practices that have been used for years by thoughtful parents. Many of these ideas have come from the staff of women and men who work with the infants of the Frank Porter Graham Child Development Center, and the ideas reflect their sensitive understanding of children. Some of the activities of the curriculum are based on games used by Piaget. Although the activities have come from many sources, no activities are used that do not fit into the four-point framework of the Carolina Infant Curriculum.

What does the organization and framework of the Curriculum mean for the parent, the caregiver, or the teacher? Far from meaning schedules and regimentation, they can mean more freedom and flexibility. The person who has a resource that is well-organized can focus most of his attention on the joy and enthusiasm of interacting with the child. The curriculum complements the parent or teacher's own good ideas. With a greater variety of ideas, the choices in parenting and teaching can become more real and satisfying.

TEACHING-LEARNING FORMAT

The specific goals of the daily program for children ages zero through four years are:

1. To provide a safe, healthful, and comfortable environment for young children. A prerequisite for good research with young children is that the children be provided a good *living* environment.

2. To provide a setting for developing, presenting, and evaluating activities which are appropriate for children ages zero through four years. Activities include those directed toward cognitive and language skills, social skills, and motor skills.

3. To provide opportunities for children to interact with peers as well as older and younger children.

4. To provide a setting for teachers to continue to learn about the behavior of children.

5. To provide settings in which individual children can interact with adults as well as participate in groups led by adults.

6. To provide observation facilities and children for study of child growth and development.

7. To establish informative and cooperative social contacts with each parent individually.

The day care program operates in a four-story building located next to a public elementary school. The program includes two settings: one setting for infants (four weeks to walking age) and one setting for one-, two-, and three-year-olds.

The day care programs comply with the state of North Carolina licens-

110

ing standards and the federal interagency guidelines for group day care programs.

Setting for Pre-walking Infants

A suite of four adjoining rooms and a large hallway make up the teaching-learning environment for infants who are not yet walking. Two of the rooms are for play and two are for sleep.

The fourteen infants in the rooms are served by a staff of four assistant teachers and a supervisor, who is also responsible for recruiting participants and maintaining parent contacts.

The infants pace themselves through their days. Thus, at no time are all fourteen infants involved in the same activities. Teachers interact individually with children as they arrive; before, during, and after each child's feeding time; and at the end of the day. Feeding occurs in the hall into which each room opens. The hall is furnished with a rug, chairs, and couches. Infants are held, while getting their bottles, and put in an infant seat or at a feeding table when they are fed solid foods.

As infants finish their morning feeding, they interact with toys, each other, or a teacher. Toys are arranged on low shelves so that infants can get the items themselves. At this time, teachers rotate among the children and present specific activities to children individually in the playrooms.

The staff meets early in the morning or late in the afternoon to discuss the children's behaviors, to record their progress, and to discuss program operations.

Each teacher is responsible for curriculum activities for three or four infants. This means that the teacher presents the activity to these particular infants, both initially and at the end of the teaching time (two to three weeks), and that he or she makes sure the infants have an opportunity to carry on their activities every day. Any other teacher, however, may engage the same children in activities. The teacher is periodically assigned the responsibility for different children.

Transition to Toddler-Preschool Setting

When infants are able to walk alone, they are gradually moved into the setting for one-, two-, and three-year-olds. A teacher from the infant program brings the infant to the toddler-preschool program for a short time each morning for one or two weeks. The time the infants stay with the older children increases gradually each day until they stay in the group all day. The familiar teacher stays with the infant at first, but gradually he begins to interact with other children; thus he allows the new teachers to get acquainted with the infant. The infants move out of infant day care in groups of three or four.

Setting for One-, Two-, and Three-Year-Olds

On another floor in the research building, a large area is divided into classes for one- and two-year olds and for one-, two-, and three-year-olds. Currently, two classes (called "houses" by the children) are set up to accomodate twenty-nine children. One house has fourteen children, with one teacher and three teacher assistants; it provides educational care for one- and two-year-olds. A second house has fifteen one-, two-, and three-year-olds, with one teacher and four assistant teachers.

Each house group has access to two areas. One tiled area (fifty feet by twenty-two feet) is set up for creative activities (art, playdough, sand, water), housekeeping or dramatic play, indoor climbing, and large building blocks. A carpeted area (twenty-four feet by eighteen feet) is used for manipulative activities involving peg boards, puzzles, small blocks, nesting toys, stack toys, and push toys. The carpeted area is used during transition times: arrival times, before lunch, after lunch on rainy days, and after naps.

Diapering is done by one teacher in each house while other teachers are involved in individual or small group activities (reading stories or helping a child with stack toys). Children's diapers are changed whenever needed, of course, but all children are diapered before lunch and after naps.

Distribution of Children

The children are "multi-age grouped" within each house. This arrangement provides the younger children with models for behaviors they will learn. It also allows older children to practice behaviors they have already learned and to help teach younger children (to hold a hand while on a walk, to push the wagon, to pick up dropped toys). The data so far indicate that children of different ages interact and that, over the course of a year, younger children increase their amounts of play with older children. On-going observational studies are looking for an optimum age mix for children in this natural environment. It may be that the modeling-teaching interchanges are more frequent when one- and three-year-olds or two- and four-year-olds are together.

The experiences a child has alone or with others at his developmental level are as important as interchanges with children of different ages. Therefore, within each house, the children are subgrouped for an hour in the morning and again in the afternoon. During these times, teachers work either with children on their assigned activity items or with three or four children who are at the same developmental level in painting or dramatic play. This arrangement insures that the younger children will have an opportunity to explore on their own without interference from older children who wish to tell younger ones what to do. Similarly, there is time for the older children to possess toys without younger ones vying for them.

Distribution of Teachers

The assigned child-to-teacher arrangement should not be interpreted to mean that children and teachers move simultaneously together through the day. The teachers within each house operate as a team. Particularly during transition times, but also during activity times, teachers work according to the zone plan, as opposed to man-to-man (LeLaurin and Risley, 1972). Under the zone plan, a teacher covers an area (a specific activity area such as a playdough table) or is the first teacher to move with children who are ready for their next program (first teacher to help children get to bed after lunch, first teacher to receive children after waking from naps). The man-to-man system would involve a teacher collecting all of his or her charges before, for example, going outside or beginning to use playdough. During activity time, teachers will seek out particular children to be sure that they have had the activity experience. In general, however, teachers stay with an activity until the next event occurs.

Routines: Eating, Napping, and Toileting

Food for an early morning snack and for lunch is prepared by the cafeteria at the adjacent public school. Arrangements have been made for the cafeteria to make substitutions in the regular school menu to assure that all food can be eaten by the youngest children. A teacher transports the food daily, in bulk, to the day care center. The older children eat family style and help themselves from bowls on the table. They pour their own milk and often pour the milk for younger children. For the older two- and three-year-olds, the family style procedure allows each child to choose how much he wants to eat. After the children have taken the amounts they want to eat, the teacher can use teaching techniques such as praise and subtle instruction to encourage them to eat more of some food if amount is a problem. This procedure developed from a study done with two-year-olds who were poor eaters (Hall and Holmberg, 1974).

The children nap on cots for two to two-and-a-half hours a day. The cots are placed in the tiled area while children are involved in activities in the carpeted area. Teachers place beds in strategic places to prevent early nappers from being disturbed by older children who come in later for naps. Teachers on duty in the nap area sit quietly by the beds of restless children until they have quieted themselves. Children leave the nap area as they awaken and go to the carpeted area where diapers are changed and a teacher is ready to engage them in activity before snacks.

Toilet training is handled in a very relaxed manner. Children begin to use the potty when they are approaching two years of age and/or parents indicate they are using the potty at home. They are put in training pants at this time. Children who frequently wet their pants after they are in their third year are checked every half hour to determine when wet pants occur. After a pattern is determined, the teacher goes with the children to the bathroom at appropriate times. Gradually, the teacher withdraws from taking the child and asks the child to go to the bathroom alone; finally, the child goes regularly by himself.

In summary, the schedule of daily activities for one-, two-, and three-year-olds is as follows:

7:45 - 9:00 (tile area)	Children arrive with parents or in cars driven by teachers. In each house, children select manipulative and cognitive materials from open shelves, engage in dramatic play, build with blocks, or use playdough until all children arrive. Some teachers work individually with children at this time on specific curriculum activities.
9:00 - 9:15 (tile area)	Morning snacks which meet the nutritional requirements for breakfast are served.
9:15 - 9:30 (tile area)	Group time is allowed for songs and finger plays.
9:30 - 10:30 (tile and carpet)	Planned experiences, which include a balance of one to one and small group activities dealing with creative (water play, graphic arts) and cognitive skills (matching objects by color or shape, labeling, stacking or aligning blocks), are begun. One week, children are assigned new curriculum items as described in written guide sheets. The following two weeks, the items are varied through the use of different materials or through incorporation of the items into different activities, but the goal of the activity is maintained. The three-week cycle is then begun again with new items.

10:30 - 11:00	Outside activities are begun.
11:00 - 11:15 (carpet area)	This is a transition time when diapers are changed and stories are read to small groups of children.
11:15 - 12:00 (tile area)	Lunch is served.
12:00 -	Faces and hands are washed. Younger children go to bed after eating and older children play outside.
12:30 -	Older children come inside for naps.
2:30 - (carpet area)	Early risers have stories read to them. All children, after diapers are changed, are involved in language activities or manipulative materials.
3:15 - (tile area)	Afternoon snacks include a fruit or vegetable, bread product, and drink.
3:30 - 5:00	Planned activities, similar to the early morning schedule, are begun. Children begin leaving for homes at 3:45.

PARENT INVOLVEMENT

The approach that is used in the parent program is to individualize contacts with parents. This approach is consistent with curriculum planning for an individual child's development of behaviors and skills. The goal of the program has been to establish open lines of communication directly with each parent rather than to attempt to organize parent groups. Perhaps, after parents feel that they are able to interact more openly with the staff, they will want to set up their own parent group. In addition to individualizing parent contacts, the program attempts to involve all teachers in parent work instead of having one staff member responsible for parent communications. The infant nursery supervisor, who is extremely capable and successful in her contacts with parents, initiates the link between parents and other teachers.

The "individualized" parent approach begins with each teacher being responsible for contacts with four children and their families. Each teacher plans an afternoon for her or his families to come to the center to see the kinds of activities children engage in, to meet other teachers and representatives from the medical staff, and to have cookies and punch. Parents are given a polaroid picture of their children which was taken while the children were engaged in an activitiy. Slides are shown of other activities that the children participate in. Parents are subsequently invited to holiday parties (which have been eagerly attended). The emphasis of these activities is on social interchange between parents, teachers, and children, as well as on individualizing parent interactions. Pictures of children have been well received by parents and are good ground breakers for helping teachers converse with parents.

Other contacts vary, depending on the parent's situation. They include home visits by the teacher with the child, telephone calls, visits to the center, and other informal meetings for chatting about school and children. Parents take the initiative with this type of contact.

STAFF DEVELOPMENT

Four premises provide the framework around which the selection of, and a training program for, the teaching staff is built.

The importance of children having teachers who represent the ethnic and cultural values of the children's home is crucial. When a child spends many hours a day in the care of persons outside his family, those who care for him have a responsibility to provide some continuity in life style and to preserve the child's cultural identity. While the goals of the program are to introduce change in the child's developmental progress, every effort should be made to emphasize the child's unique *family heritage.* Day care should not be in the business of homogenizing children in our society.

The importance of staff being involved in applied studies directly relevant to everyday teaching procedures is essential. In a research center, it is important to maintain communication and good relations between the teaching staff and the research staff. One way to develop the necessary cooperative interchanges is to provide opportunities for teachers themselves to determine the important questions to be asked regarding the child's behavior patterns and classroom management procedures. Questions related to these areas easily come out in staff discussions, either of particular children or of the program's organization.

A related guideline for staff development is the importance of staff opportunities to develop skills in analyzing child behaviors. These skills include defining the child behaviors that are of interest in the program, observing those behaviors under specified conditions, and altering teaching procedures to help children acquire the desired behaviors. Learning these skills can become part of the teaching as well as part of the staff development program.

A program which emphasizes the growth and development of children as individuals must place great importance on its approach to staff training. Staff members also need individual attention. Those concerned with organizing and planning research, development, and teaching programs should plan staff learning programs that focus on each teacher's particular skill levels.

General Staffing Procedures

The current staff includes one supervising teacher and four teacher assistants in infant day care, and one head teacher, one associate teacher, and five assistant teachers in the toddler day care program. All teachers are employees of the state of North Carolina. Fair labor practices, employee benefits, and salary scales are overseen by the University of North Carolina Personnel Office.

In planning the yearly schedule for the children, provision is made for two, one-week workshops for teachers, one in August and one in March. Children do not attend the day care program during these two weeks, nor on state holidays. Provision is also made for staff to attend in-state and out-of-state professional meetings and workshops, and national conferences and conventions on the education of young children. These meetings provide opportunities for teachers to meet and interact with other day care teachers, to hear presentations by leaders in the field of child development, and to recognize the importance of their jobs as teachers of young children.

Implementing Staff Development On-Site

Regular staff meetings are necessary to operate a comprehensive day care program. Communication with staff is crucial in a program which endeavors to combine research, development, and teaching. Finding meeting times which are convenient for all the staff is no easy task in a day care program. When all children are napping, however, most staff can attend meetings. Student helpers provide supervision of children who awaken before the one-hour meeting is over. Three group meetings are planned weekly.

Specific Curriculum Meetings

A member of the curriculum development staff meets with the teaching staff every week. Specific curriculum assignments for children are made every third week. During the third week meeting, new activities are demonstrated and materials necessary for activities are discussed. The two meetings between activity assignment weeks are used to get feedback from teachers on the success with which activities are being implemented.

Specific teaching techniques are also discussed and demonstrated during these meetings. Discussions at the meetings, which emphasize the teachers' participation in the development of activities by curriculum staff, are important communication links between the teachers and the research staff.

Child Behavior and Management Meetings

The staffs meet weekly to discuss the problems and progress of individual children. These meetings emphasize the social interactions children have with teachers and other children, and the general management procedures operating in the classroom. The staff discussions at these meetings have resulted in teachers identifying specific teacher behaviors that concern them, and consequently identifying specific teacher behaviors that help the child learn appropriate behaviors. An example of the outcome of these sessions is described in an article, "How Teacher Talk Creates Child Chatter" (Holmberg, Hall, and Passey, 1974). The paper describes teachers' concerns about the small amount of talking a child did at school and their successful plan to rephrase their questions to the child in order to increase her talking at school.

Observations of child behavior are sometimes made by the teachers themselves and sometimes by student assistants. The meetings are opportunities for teachers to get peer feedback in the form of observations about children's progress as well as their own progress in helping the children develop desired patterns of behavior.

An example of the general management problem identified by teachers is reported in an article by Hall and Holmberg (1974) on the ways teachers can help children learn to eat a little of *all* their food at lunchtime. (This study and others were referred to earlier in describing the procedures during lunch and naptime in the day care program.)

Over time, these applied studies result in teachers developing a repertoire of techniques which are successful under specified conditions.

Planning Meetings

The third weekly meeting integrates the results of discussion in the two previous meetings (described previously) into a general plan for the upcoming week. The lead teachers work out a daily schedule with the total staff. Weekly responsibilities are assigned for transporting children, setting up areas for eating snacks and lunch, and arranging areas for napping. The staff also decides how specific curriculum activities will be implemented. During the meetings, the teachers try to ensure that each day will be well-

TABLE 3

EVALUATION PROCEDURES

MEASUREMENT DEVICE	PURPOSE	WHEN USED	WHICH CHILDREN
INTELLECTUAL DEVELOPMENT			
1. BAYLEY SCALES OF INFANT DEVELOPMENT A. MENTAL DEVELOPMENT INDEX B. PSYCHOMOTOR DEVELOPMENT INDEX C. INFANT BEHAVIOR RECORD	1. TO OTBAIN A NORMATIVE MEASURE OF THE CHILD'S INTELLECTUAL STATUS	1. 3, 6, 9, 12, & 18 MONTHS	1. EXPERIMENTAL AND CONTROL
2. STANFORD-BINET INTELLIGENCE SCALE	2. TO OBTAIN A NORMATIVE MEASURE OF THE CHILD'S INTELLECTUAL STATUS	2. 24, 36, 48, & 60 MONTHS	2. EXPERIMENTAL AND CONTROL
3. UZGIRIS-HUNT ORDINAL SCALES OF DEVELOPMENT	3. TO OBTAIN MEASURES OF: A. VISUAL PURSUIT AND PERMANENCE OF OBJECTS B. DEVELOPMENT OF MEANS FOR ACHIEVING DESIRED ENVIRON-MENTAL ENDS C. DEVELOPMENT OF SCHEMAS IN RELATION TO OBJECTS D. DEVELOPMENT OF CAUSALITY E. THE CONSTRUCTION OF OBJECTS IN SPACE F. DEVELOPMENT OF IMITATION	3. 15 MONTHS	3. EXPERIMENTAL AND CONTROL
4. McCARTHY SCALES OF CHILDREN'S ABILITIES (VERBAL INDEX)	4. TO OBTAIN A MEASURE OF VERBAL COMPETENCE	4. 42, 54, & 66 MONTHS	4. EXPERIMENTAL AND CONTROL
5. AUDITORY AND VISUAL HABITUATION	5. TO OBTAIN A MEASURE OF ATTENTIONAL BEHAVIOR	5. 6 TIMES YEARLY BETWEEN 6 WEEKS & 60 MONTHS	5. EXPERIMENTAL AND CONTROL
6. INSTRUMENTAL LEARNING	6. TO OBTAIN MEASURES OF LEARNING SPEED AND STYLE	6. YEARLY	6. EXPERIMENTAL AND CONTROL
SOCIAL DEVELOPMENT			
1. HALF-HOUR VIDEOTAPES OF MOTHER-CHILD INTERACTIONS IN A FREE PLAY SITUATION	1. TO EXAMINE THE COURSE OF EARLY SOCIAL DEVELOPMENT	1. 6, 20, 34, & 48 MONTHS	1. EXPERIMENTAL AND CONTROL
2. TIME SAMPLES OF CLASSROOM BEHAVIOR	2. TO DESCRIBE THE ECOLOGY OF THE CLASSROOM	2. YEARLY	2. EXPERIMENTAL
3. TEACHER-PARENT-CHILD INTERACTIONS IN A LABCRATORY SITUATION	3. TO ASSESS THE STRENGTH OF THE CHILD'S ATTACHMENT TO HIS/HER TEACHERS & MOTHER	3. PERIODICALLY	3. EXPERIMENTAL

balanced in terms of the nature of activities (individual and group, quiet and active, teacher-structured and self-directed) and that activities represent areas of physical, social, creative, and cognitive growth. Emphasis at this meeting is on specifying the purpose of each activity as well as on planning for the activity's implementation.

Individual Staff Conferences

A competency checklist is used as the basis for discussing the progress of the teacher. Both the teacher and the supervisor fill out the checklist prior to the meeting. The checklist includes thirty statements relating to the

TABLE 3 CONTINUED

MEASUREMENT DEVICE	PURPOSE	WHEN USED	WHICH CHILDREN
BIOLOGICAL DEVELOPMENT 1. PRENATAL & BIRTH RECORDS	1. TO INSURE BIOLOGICAL INTEGRITY UPON ADMISSION TO PROJECT	1. AT BIRTH	1. EXPERIMENTAL AND CONTROL
2. ANTHROPOMETRIC MEASURES	2. TO MONITOR PHYSICAL GROWTH & DEVELOPMENT	2. 2, 6, 9, 18, 24, 36, & 48 MONTHS	2. EXPERIMENTAL AND CONTROL
3. THROAT CULTURE FOR VIRUSES, BACTERIA & MYCOPLASMAS	3. TO DETERMINE THE ETIOLOGIC AGENTS CAUSING RESPIRATORY DISEASE	3. EVERY 2 WEEKS WHEN CHILD IS WELL & DURING EACH ILLNESS	3. EXPERIMENTAL
CURRICULUM EVALUATION 1. OBSERVATIONS & OPINIONS BY RESEARCHER & TEACHERS ON EACH CURRICULUM ITEM	1. TO DETERMINE HOW SUCCESSFULLY THE CURRICULUM IS BEING IMPLEMENTED	1. DAILY	1. EXPERIMENTAL
PARENTAL ATTITUDES 1. PARENTAL ATTITUDE RESEARCH INSTRUMENT	1. TO OBTAIN AN ASSESSMENT OF MOTHERS' ATTITUDES TOWARD CHILDREARING	1. 6, 18, & 42 MONTHS	1. EXPERIMENTAL AND CONTROL
2. ROTTER'S INTERNALITY-EXTERNALITY SCALE	2. TO DETERMINE HOW MUCH IN CONTROL OF THEIR LIVES MOTHERS FEEL	2. 6, 18, & 42 MONTHS	2. EXPERIMENTAL AND CONTROL
3. SCHAEFER & ARONSON'S INFANT BEHAVIOR INVENTORY	3. TO DETERMINE TEACHERS' & PARENTS' ATTITUDES TOWARD THE CHILDREN	3. 12, 24 & 36 MONTHS	3. EXPERIMENTAL AND CONTROL
4. SCHAEFER'S CHILD BEHAVIOR WITH PARENT INVENTORY	4. TO DETERMINE HOW THE MOTHER PERCEIVES HER CHILD'S RELATIONSHIP TO HER	4. 15, 30 & 42 MONTHS	4. EXPERIMENTAL AND CONTROL
5. SPARLING/CAMPBELL OPINION SURVEY	5. TO DETERMINE PARENTAL EXPECTATIONS FOR THEIR CHILDREN	5. 9 MONTHS	5. EXPERIMENTAL AND CONTROL
HOME ENVIRONMENT 1. CALDWELL'S HOME OBSERVATION FOR MEASUREMENT OF THE ENVIRONMENT	1. TO DESCRIBE THE CHILD'S HOME ENVIRONMENT	1. 6, 18, 30, & 42 MONTHS	1. EXPERIMENTAL AND CONTROL

teacher's interchanges with children, preparation for teaching, interaction with other staff, and responsibilities at different times during the daily program.

The individual conferences are set up to obtain information from each teacher about his or her concerns with any aspect of the program and to get suggestions about ways to solve any current problems. The meetings also provide time to give teachers feedback from observations that have been made of their behaviors. Examples of behaviors that teachers have worked on include increasing the use of descriptive content words (wiggly lines, bright colors, geometric patterns) in talking to children about their art or block-building activities, the use of eye contact (getting down so the child can see a face) when talking to children rather than talking from a distance, and the use of "wh" questions (starting with *who, what, why, when* and *where* rather than with *do, are you,* or *can you)* to increase child verbalizations. A child can answer a "do you" question with a head shake, but has to answer a "wh" question with at least one word. Teachers' progress in these areas is often charted graphically so that the teacher has visual evidence of how he/she is doing.

EVALUATION AND RESEARCH

Evaluation and research within the Abecedarian Project can be classified within the following six major areas:

1. Curriculum effectiveness
2. Intellectual development of the children
3. Social development of the children
4. Biological development
5. Attitudes of parents
6. Home environment

An important function of curriculum evaluation is to provide corrective feedback while the curriculum materials are still in a formative stage. Before a new curriculum activity or item is finished, formative evaluation data are gathered to measure the effectiveness of the activity. Ratings are made by both the teacher and an observer when the child first begins an activity and again approximately three weeks later. Through the use of multiple criteria, the decision is made to accept, modify, or reject the activity as a part of the Carolina Infant Curriculum.

Any program adopting this curriculum might want to focus on basic areas of evaluation such as: (1) degree of implementation, (2) change in teacher or parent interest, and (3) change in the quality and/or quantity of child-adult interaction. When the direction of evaluation in these areas makes it seem appropriate, a program can move on to the evaluation of child progress.

A summary of the other major measurement devices used in each of these six areas is presented in Table 3. In addition to these instruments (which are administered periodically), a variety of prototypic experiments are conducted to test basic assumptions upon which the project is premised.

FUTURE PLANS

During the next two years, the Carolina Abecedarian Project plans to admit two more cohorts of 28 children each. This admission will bring the total number of children enrolled in the project to 112, with 56 each in the experimental and control groups. The current plan is to monitor these children's developmental progress at least until they are in public grade school.

Through a contract with the Northwest Child Development Council, a procedure to train teachers in the use of the Carolina Infant Curriculum is currently being developed and tested at a field site in North Carolina. When the contract is completed, this field site will provide regional demonstration and training in the use of this curriculum. Other methods for disseminating the Carolina Infant Curriculum in the western or Appalachian region of North Carolina are being explored with the North Carolina Office for Children.

BIBLIOGRAPHY

Hall, J. S., and Holmberg, M. C. The effects of teacher behaviors and food serving arrangements on young children's eating in a day care center. *Child Care Quarterly,* 1974, 3, 97-108.

Lelaurin, K., and Risley, T. R. The organization of day care environments: "Zone" versus "man-to-man" staff assignments. *Journal of Applied Behavior Analysis,* 1972, 5, 225-232.

Tyler, R. W. *Basic principles of curriculum and instruction.* Chicago: University of Chicago Press, 1950.

CHAPTER 8

Intervention Programs for Children Under Three Years

M. H. Jones

The first pre-nursery unit at UCLA came into being in 1949 (Jones, et al., 1962) at the request of parents of young, physically handicapped children (mainly those with cerebral palsy) who felt that the traditionally provided therapy program was not satisfactory. Children had not adjusted or cooperated well with therapists under the pressure of short-term, out-patient appointments. Parents felt that longer sessions on a daily basis would be more useful.

After several years experience with this pilot project, which involved only therapists, it became evident that parents were placing most of their emphasis on therapy rather than overall child development. Thus, when funding became available through the Los Angeles County United Cerebral Palsy Association and a pre-nursery unit was established at the Children's Hospital, a teacher was added to the staff in order to show the need to integrate overall development with specific therapy in this program. The therapists served as consultants to the teacher; they taught her specific, individualized techniques to be used in the classroom just as they taught parents to carry out instructions in the home training program.

In 1955, the unit at UCLA was transformed (under the author's direction) into a demonstration, research, and training unit in the Department of Pediatrics (Jones, et al., 1962). As children with different types of handicaps (physical, behavioral, and learning problems) were referred to the unit, the composition of the pre-nursery group was expanded to in-

MARGARET H. JONES is an Emeritus Professor of Pediatrics at UCLA. Her major professional interest is in the diagnosis and management of infants and young children with delayed development.

124

clude not only the severely multiply handicapped but also the autistic, the deaf/blind, those with Down's Syndrome, and others who, in the opinion of the parents and staff, could profit from the program. Normal children were not regularly enrolled but came at times as visitors. As the program developed, the staff was enlarged to include social workers and consultants in psychiatry, psychology, and orthopedics as well as in pediatrics and pediatric-neurology.

When, in 1972, this unit became a member of the consortium developed by the National United Cerebral Palsy Association , supplemental funding made it possible to document some of the procedures previously initiated and to continue to work out innovations. Also, there was considerable interchange between the staffs of this unit and other members of the consortium. A number of very helpful workshops were planned for the staffs in which all of the consortium members met together. Observation of other programs, again made possible through the Collaborative Infants Project, led to changes in the UCLA unit, particularly the initiation of a new program involving mothers and infants together in group sessions for one to two hours a day, one to two times a week.

As of 1974, three types of programs were operating at UCLA: (1) A pre-nursery unit was operated for about twelve one-and-one-half- to three-year-olds, (four to five days/week from 9:00 to 12:30). The unit was mainly for those with multiple handicaps of various types and degrees of severity. Some had behavioral problems such as autism, Down's syndrome, or other genetic, congenital, or metabolic abnormalities which lead to developmental delay. (2) Mother-infant group sessions were held twice weekly in the afternoons for about two hours each. The sessions served about eight mother-child units. (3) Home training (therapist, teacher), especially for infants from birth to ten months, was provided, with individual sessions weekly to monthly, depending on the need and distance from the center that the family lived. (The home training program served about fifteen to twenty children, from birth to three months of age.)

Children were referred from private physicians, clinics, agencies, and individuals. Intake began with the physician's review of records submitted and medical evaluation. Following this review, the teacher interviewed the parent(s) and evaluated the child; then the therapists examined the child. The social worker was a member of the clinic-conference team which met together with parents and child to review evaluations made and consider types of programs appropriate. She or he made these individual consultation appointments with parents as requested and also made occasional home visits. If the children were admitted to the pre-nursery or mother/child group programs, the social worker invited the mothers to join informal discussion sessions which she or he led (Posner, 1973).

GOALS AND OBJECTIVES

Initially, the goals of the program were traditional ones concerned mainly with therapeutic management of physical (sensory-motor) disabilities. Gradually, the goals came to involve a trans-disciplinary approach (medical/educational model) to remediation of handicaps.

Overall Objectives

(1) Objectives, to be obtained for the child and family, beginning as soon after birth as delay in development (or probable delay) was identified and the child referred, were:

   (a) Medical, educational psychological evaluation followed by periodic (total staff with parents) re-evaluation at approximately three-month intervals for those enrolled in a continuing program.

   (b) Development of an individualized management-training program including assistance to family members in respect to their feelings about themselves and the child.

(2) Objectives for research were:

   (a) Development of innovative techniques and equipment to meet special needs. (See section entitled "Teaching-Learning Format.)

   (b) Development of ways of measuring changes in socialization (Rogers, et al.).

(3) Objectives for training were:

   (a) Professional staff already in the unit to receive training through the university extension and other lecture series; through special seminars, conferences and meetings with professional visitors; and through staff attendance at professional meetings.

   (b) Students of various types (such as physicians, nurses, social workers, psychologists, child developmentalists and others) to receive training.

   (c) Visual aids and other material to be developed for use in the unit and for dissemination.

TEACHING-LEARNING FORMAT

On the basis of child development principles and through a Piagetian approach, the long term goals were developed, obviously, to make it possible for each child to achieve his maximal potential in all areas. One of the greatest problems in establishing specific long term goals for the very young, multihandicapped child was (and is) *our* lack of sufficient knowledge to make accurate predictions about the child's development at a very early age. An early prognosis, especially if given by a person "in authority" (e.g., a physician), has a profound effect on the handling of the child by the parents and other professionals and hence on the overall outcome.

After as accurate an evaluation as possible was made in all areas, short term objectives which were achievable in a short period of time were developed. Little steps, one at a time, were basic to achievement.

In the UCLA program, weekly staff-parent conferences provided an opportunity for the sharing of results of evaluations (both formal and informal) made prior to and during the sessions. Parents and staff posed questions, shared feelings, and together set specific goals and objectives. In the initial conference for each child referred, the staff and the parents considered the various programs available and together worked out a management plan. If the child was enrolled in the pre-nursery or mother/child groups program, total staff-parent reviews were scheduled at approximately three-month intervals.

The pre-nursery program emphasized personality development. It provided an opportunity for the child to explore, with appropriate intervention, a low key, quiet, happy relaxed atmosphere with the teacher as the pivotal person. The program was designed to integrate treatment of the physical aspects of problems into all aspects of the child's life. This required trans-disciplinary cooperation on the part of all members of the professional staff.

In our trans-disciplinary approach to the program, all professionals were responsible for a number of areas. They were responsible for expertise in their fields. They were required to enter into staff-parent planning sessions to determine the best way to accomplish objectives in their special areas, within the framework of the child's daily activities. All professionals were expected to learn appropriate ways from teachers to motivate each child for the desired activity. Evaluation of each child by professionals in his or her area of speciality was also expected. Teaching other professionals and parents specific techniques and supervising both the other professionals and parents in performance of these techniques was also required.

The structure of the pre-nursery program included the following areas: (1) mother/child interaction, (2) socialization in peer relationships for young children, (3) learning experiences in an educationally-based structure, and (4) individualized treatment procedures which included physical, occupational, language and speech therapy in a trans-disciplinary approach.

Parents brought their children into the classroom where they were greeted by the teacher. Because the first half hour was a critical time for adjustment for the child, a quiet, peaceful, happy atmosphere in the classroom was the goal, and crying was usually at a minimum. Also, so the child would not be confronted with the need to adjust to many adults, one teacher and one therapist were assigned to each child as the major intervenors for that child. When first admitted to the pre-nursery unit, the parents usually remained in the classroom for a short time, and then gradually withdrew to watch behind a one-way mirror until the child became familiar with the staff and surroundings.

Flow Pattern of Program Activities

Activities were geared to provide *play experiences* for the children enrolled. The staff quietly, unobtrusively reinforced positive behavior and intervened if negative activities, for example, hitting or hair pulling, became a problem. The flow pattern of the nursery day is outlined in the following pages.

A schedule of activities was followed daily to give children a sense of stability and time sequence. Flexibility was considered a built-in component so that the school program could be "custom tailored" to fit individual needs of the children.

The Schedule

9:00 A.M.

ARRIVAL

Parents bring their children to school. On arrival, children are encouraged to put their wraps and lunch boxes into their own lockers. Assistance is given by the teacher and/or parent according to individual need.

Objective: that each child will develop self-help skills according to his capabilities and the feeling of being independent.

PLAY PERIOD

Children are encouraged and given the opportunity to select on their own from a variety of materials and activities. Gesturing, head nodding, and eye movements are acceptable indicators of choice. If the child cannot move himself to the material or activity, the teacher helps him to get there. Mobile children are expected to move to their choices and verbalization is encouraged.

Objective: (1) that the child will select and become involved with a variety of materials made available to him in the classroom

(2) that the child will interact with at least one other child

9:45—10:00 A.M.

BATHROOMING

Toileting time can become an excellent opportunity for children to socialize. Interacting with an adult during the diapering process, accepting handling by an adult other than his mother, and viewing himself in a mirror (placed above the diapering table) are effective ways to build self-concept and body-image.

Toilet training is an integral part of the nursery school program; teachers and other staff members work in cooperation with parents as the child indicates readiness.

Objective: (1) that the child will interact with the adult caring for him (in diapering or toileting) in a cooperative manner

(2) that the child will move toward learning to indicate need for toileting and, so far as physically possible, care for his own toileting (washing hands and handling clothing)

(3) that the child will begin to note sex differences

10:00—10:30 A.M.

JUICE TIME

This is a good time for the therapist and the teacher to work together in helping the child with feeding. Oral pharyngeal techniques are employed here. It is also a socializing time for the children and an opportunity to copy others who are managing the feeding process quite well on their own.

Objective: (1) that the child learn to feed himself as independently as possible

(2) that the child learn to accept help from others (e.g., therapy techniques)

(3) that the child vocalize or verablize with other children and/or adults

(4) that the child learn self-help skills (e.g., getting and putting away bib, handling drinking cup, taking crackers, mixing pudding, etc.)

10:30—10:45 A.M.

OUTDOOR PLAY TIME (GETTING READY)

The children are expected to get to the "train" (a special vehicle for moving children out to the play yard) by crawling, scooting, or walking with assistance or on their own, with only the minimum of adult help needed. This practice is to help build independence as well as to motivate the children to move.

The children are encouraged to climb into the train on their own.

Objective: (1) that the child build self-help skills by getting his own wrap from his locker (if possible for him to do so) or indicate to an adult that it is needed

(2) that the child be motivated to move toward the train on his own volition

10:45—11:30 A.M.

OUTDOOR PLAY

Teachers pull the train to the outdoor area. The variety of shrubs and flowers give opportunity for touching, smelling, and picking. Awareness of the environment through the senses of sight, sound, and touch are developed through many sensory experiences offered outdoors. Wheel toys, swings, sandbox, jungle-gym, water, plastic containers, etc. are readily available to the children. The terrain has a variety of sloping levels with concrete paths, grassy areas, and low tree stumps for climbing and pulling up or cruising activities.

Objective: that the child orient himself spatially in the outdoor environment through:
exploring the yard with whatever adult help is required
exploring and using the equipment in a sensory-motor way
interacting with other children and the adults

11:30—11:45 A.M.

Therapists join the teachers in the outdoor area and here again therapy and educational program combine as a successful intervention for helping these handicapped children find out about themselves and the world in which they live.

11:45—12:30

LUNCH TIME

(Refer to Juice Time)

Objective: (1) that the child experience a variety of textures and taste in foods

(2) that the child learn to manage his eating as independently as is possible for him

Each child brings a lunch box from home with food prepared by the mother. Frequently pudding, soup, or another type of easily prepared food is made at school by the children and teachers.

12:30—2:00 P.M.*

NAP TIME

Most of the children enrolled in the program stay for an afternoon nap.

---

*As the program developed, it was modified. Children went home after lunch; thus space and staff time were provided for additional groups of children in the afternoon.

Objective: (1) that the child become accustomed to wearing braces and other appliances during sleep if these are needed

(2) that the child have greater sequence to his day. (Some children travel distances to come to school. Leaving right after lunch sometimes means a delayed or shortened nap which is disrupting to some children.)

(3) that the parent learn techniques of handling or introducing their child to appliances needed to be worn during sleep

Naptime offers a quiet end to a busy morning at school. This is often a time when children socialize with each other as they get ready for bed and on getting up and waiting for parents to come to pick them up.

2:30 P.M.

DISMISSAL

Here is a good time for teachers to communicate with the parents regarding the child, answer parents' questions, or set a time for a conference. It is a good opportunity to observe mother(father)-child interaction and relationship.

Open communication with the parent is a must if the school program is to make an effective difference for the children.

As suggested in the flow pattern, activities involving language and speech stimulation were carried on by all members of the team. The teacher talked to the children quietly, gave short, clear directions for various activities and allowed each child *time to respond in his own fashion* to the request or command.

Special Programs

(1) *Oral-pharyngeal development, pre-school evaluation, and feeding training.* Although many techniques were tried, the greatest successes appeared to result from the approach developed by Helen Mueller. (Mueller, 1973)

(2) *Pool activities.* These were possible through the assistance of vol-

unteers working under the staff's supervision. The objectives were to provide opportunities for the children to become comfortable in a warm pool, to sit, to walk, to splash, and perhaps to learn to swim. Special equipment was designed to hook over the side of a therapeutic pool to give seating and parallel bars of appropriate dimensions. For some children, the time in the pool was the happiest, most active part of the program. (Kehr, 1974)

(3) *Special techniques.* The following tools were used particularly with reference to language stimulation, but they were also useful for physical and educational development.

Play Test: This is an individual play technique designed to explore an infant's discriminative, receptive language abilities and use of hands. The equipment used in the play test was found to work well with infants under one year of age. It was placed in the child's crib at home and permitted him to choose between two auditory stimuli. In studies by Friedlander (1968, 1970) and Cyruble-Jacobs (1975), severely handicapped infants demonstrated greater frequency and longer duration of listening than did normal children; they clearly distinguished between hum and Sesame Street songs.

Cyber-Go-Round: Pictures used with this equipment were gathered by both parents and team members. They represented items in the child's environment which were meaningful to him/her.

Three switches, which were color coded, allowed even a severely physically handicapped child to operate the carousel (Cyber-Go-Round) by making it go forward, back, or stop. Much vocalizing, eye contact, and hand movement occured spontaneously. (Kafafian, 1972)

Learning Box: This item was used to reward (by ringing a bell) certain behavior in a play situation. Its aim was to encourage eye fixation and left to right following by using sequentially illuminated lights. The equipment was developed to promote head holding in a upright position. A centrally placed, easily operated switch allowed the child to stop the progression and gave him a non-vocal means of answering a question.

Sensory Story: This is an activity designed to encourage discrimination of tactile-kinesthetic feedback and language development on an individual basis. It offered an opportunity for the teacher/therapist to talk to the child and have the time to listen to his/her way of communicating, whether by actual expressive language by behavior. (Barrett, 1967, and Jones, et al., 1969) 1969)

Confined Space: A small area with plain walls five feet high (developed in Dallas) was arranged so that there were about two-and-one-half square feet per person. Scarves and a few soft toys were the only objects in the area. This activity encouraged body contact and vocalization/babbling and self-initiated talking. The procedure was carefully monitored by the teacher who was in the area with the children. He or she used a special record form to measure progress against an initial baseline on which she recorded children's behavior in the group. (Barrett, 1967 and Jones, 1969)

Theraplay: This was developed by a physical therapist to promote spontaneous activity to develop balance and motor planning. It was, subsequently, found to increase peer interaction in a more normal way than was possible in the classroom. It consisted of a separate enclosed environment completely covered on the inside with resilient material. Thus, it was safe for children to explore (and fall down in without fear of injury).

Format for Mother/Child Interaction Groups

The format for the mother/child group sessions, which lasted about two hours once or twice a week, had the same overall objectives as the pre-nursery unit format. Because of the shorter sessions, the program consisted almost entirely of assisting the mothers in their own handling of the children. Once a week, as was true for the pre-nursery unit also, for approximately three quarters of an hour the mothers had the option of participating in a group discussion or meeting the social worker. During this time, the children were with the staff. If possible, the younger children (ten-eighteen months) formed one group, and the older children (eighteen-thirty-six months) another.

Home Training Program

The home training program was a more traditional program in which, following total staff-parent evaluation, the assigned therapist-teacher reviewed with the mother and child, on a weekly to monthly basis, a home training program. Initially, home training was a therapist-child program. Gradually, the teachers became more involved. Unfortunately, time did not allow very much home visiting, but we believe it would have been helpful.

PARENT INVOLVEMENT

Parents were heavily involved in this program and were considered by the staff to be part of the team. Specifically they were involved in the following:

(a) In total staff conferences at three-month intervals
(b) In the home training program as major agents
(c) Weekly mothers' discussion groups (optional)
(d) Monthly PTA type of parent meetings (evenings—some educational, some social, some related to fund raising for the school)
(e) Classroom work under the teacher's direction
(f) Regularly scheduled individual conferences with teacher and with therapist
(g) Informal interaction with other mothers whose children were enrolled in programs
(h) Group and/or individual participation in fund raising to support the unit

FACTORS IN SELECTION OF STAFF

Teachers. The teachers in our program were expected to have knowledge of normal infants and young children. They were able to relate to parents, individually and in groups, and to teach them appropriate techniques and approaches in handling and training their children. They were also expected to be able to work closely with other professionals. This meant that teachers had to record and convey to physicians, therapists, social workers, and psychologists the objective observations, problems, and questions derived from their work with the children. (The physician especially needed to have the teacher's written, concrete observations regarding the child's behavior, gross and fine motor performance, attention span, and any abnormal episodes that might have been some type of seizure.)

It meant, further, that the teachers were open to learning specific recommended procedures, to carrying them out in the classroom, and to integrating them into the child's daily activities.

Particularly in working with parents, therapists, social workers, and psychologists, the teacher needed to be concerned with identifying optional approaches (on an individual basis) for motivating the children—approaches that could be used consistently in the pre-nursery, therapy, and home training programs.

Patience to *wait* for the child, particularly the child with physical and/or emotional handicaps, to initiate activity, to make choices, and, if the child needed help to start an activity, the patience to assist him were expected of our teachers.

Medical Personnel. A pediatrician, particularly one with knowledge of normal child development and an interest in infants and young children with deviations from normal development, was needed. He or she had to have some training and experience in neurological problems common to this age group as well as in congenital and genetic abnormalities. Because of the frequency of visual and auditory deficits and abnormal oral-pharyngeal functions, physicians had to test infants and young children carefully and repeatedly for possible deficits in this areas. These duties allowed the pediatrician to serve as coordinator for the various health problems to be considered and to make appropriate referrals.

Also, the pediatrician was expected to be interested in working with the teachers, in providing them with guidelines in respect to the child's medical problems as they related to learning and to classroom activities, and in requesting from the teachers the objective written reports of the child's achievement as well as of his problems. Often handicapped children present a very poor appearance in a medical office or clinic and do not demonstrate either their ability to learn or their maximal gross and fine motor skills. Moreover, direct communication with them may be difficult for they tend to become tense and withdrawn.

Orthopedists. The orthopedic consultant at this unit was interested in total rehabilitation of the young child and conducted monthly orthopedic conferences with parents, pediatrician, therapist, and the social worker staff that was present. Thus, an opportunity for direct interchange of observations and open discussion was provided.

Psychiatrist. The pediatric psychiatrist was of great importance in consultation in regards to individual children referred by staff for evaluation. He was also involved in regularly planned conferences with social workers,

136

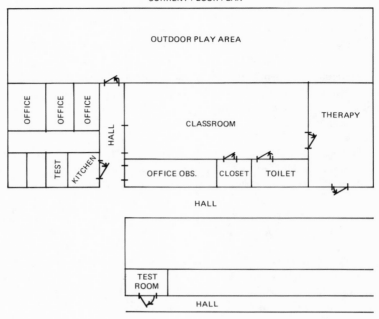

FIGURE 1
CURRENT FLOOR PLAN

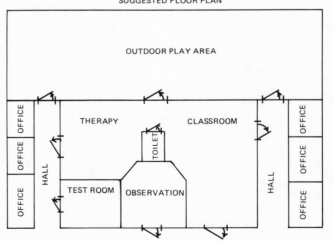

FIGURE 2
SUGGESTED FLOOR PLAN

therapists, and psychologists.

Staff Therapists, Social Workers and Psychologists. This group was expected to have: (1) knowledge of normal child development; (2) interest in learning techniques from teachers, particularly ways of motivating children; (3) an ability to teach specific procedures to teachers and parents, not just to treat the child on a one to one basis, (4) patience to wait for the child's response and sit back and observe a child's abilities *before* intervening.

Volunteers. The volunteers were given orientation, training, specific duties, and continuing supervision by staff. They were expected to have an overall interest in young children, a good physical condition enabling them to handle children, ability to learn, and reliability in carrying out specific instructions.

ADMINISTRATIVE CONSIDERATIONS

Space. The facility provided the following things (as illustrated in Figure 1): classroom, therapy area, toilet training room, storage, observation room-office area with one-way mirror and intercom, separate individual test/training area, and offices. Larger conference rooms were available on scheduling.

On the basis of experience with the program, a suggested design plan was drawn up (Figure 2). This space arrangement preserved the possibility of easy interchange between therapists and teachers but provided a larger observation area from which more activities could be seen.

The facility was in use full time. The staff, optimally, involved a head teacher and two other trained teachers, therapists (physical, occupational, and speech therapists, each at least half-time), a social worker at least half-time, a secretary at least half-time, and a consulting psychologist, pediatrician-neurologist, orthopedist, and child psychiatrist. The ratio of adult to child in the pre-nursery unit was 1:2.

The cost per child varied, depending upon the number of children in the different programs. For a total case load of forty children, the average cost per child was about $2,000 per year. Volunteers played a very significant role in direct service and in providing funding for the program (Fig. 3).

EVALUATION

Socialization Scale for Children (Figure 4). Because no scales were avail-

138

FIGURE 3

Funding for the UCLA Infant Intervention Program

		Auspices	Funds
1949-54	Pilot Program	Private non-profit	Patient fees
1954	Community Health Facility	Children's Hospital	U.C.P.–L.A.C.
1955	UCLA	Department of Pediatrics project (research, training, and development project)	U.C.P.–L.A.C. patient fees, U.C.P. Collaborative Infant Project and other donations State Department of Education (Deaf-Blind Program)

able to record socialization behavior of very young children and because of the importance of such documentation for program planning, a study was set-up to design and apply a socialization inventory. Specific behaviors were identified: the child (1) moves away from the environment, (2) stays to him/herself, (3) moves out to adults, (4) moves out to peers, (5) moves out to materials, and (6) overall state of child. Recorded observations with seven children, ages twenty to thirty-seven months, enrolled in a prenursery for handicapped children, provided a profile of each child. Interater reliability between trained observers was good (97%).

Other Measures. The following means were also used in the UCLA program:

A. The Denver Development Screening Test

B. A narrative, prepared by the teacher

C. Records of physical development and oral pharyngeal development prepared by therapists

D. Individualized records of objectives and training procedures used by staff and parents and reports of what was accomplished for each child.

Mother Groups. In evaluating our effectiveness with mothers, we found that the mothers typically went through a number of stages in development during the year: testing, acceptance and clarification of feelings, a move away from themselves to school needs, confidence gained in themselves, and a fear of the future with the change to a new facility at the end of the year. All parents attending these groups filled in a questionnaire.

Follow-up Study—1962. Sixty-four children who had attended the pre-nursery were followed. The report which appeared in the *Journal of American Medical Women's Association* described the results of the study.

> Diagnosis of cerebral palsy at a mean age of 2 yrs. 5 mo. was consistent with that on re-examination at mean age of 6 yrs. 11 mo., with few exceptions.
> The educational status of 56 children followed at mean period of 44 months after leaving the nursery revealed 63 per cent educable (13 per cent in regular schools, 50 per cent in schools for handicapped, 34 per cent not educable, and 3 per cent who died).
> Progressive increases in I.Q. from 60-70 to 95-100 in 4 of the 9 for whom ratings during and after nursery are available suggested the need for further study of the role of the pre-nursery in intellectual development.
> The use of scales of skills, consisting of selected items from Gesell and Vineland scales, to compare developmental status during pre-nursery school with that at follow-up indicated: (1) significantly higher language quotients at follow-up, (2) significantly lower locomotor quotients at follow-up, and (3) no significant change in self-help or personal-social areas.
> Intelligence did not appear to be a major determinant in developmental progress as measured on the scales of skills employed.
> Retrospectively, most parents believed that they had made real gains in understanding during the pre-nursery period; a few parents of slow learning children considered that the unit provided too much pressure for the children and too much encouragement for them (Jones, et al., 1962).

FUTURE PLANS

In July 1974, A. H. Parmelee, M.D., assumed overall directorship of the unit with Judy Howard, M.D., being directly in charge. Some changes have been instituted in the focus and format of the program.

Figure 4

Item Description
Socialization Inventory

A. MOVES AWAY

1. Hides, turns away
    The child puts his hands over his face, closes eyes, goes behind furniture, goes behind an adult or child, turns his head or body away from the situation. (He may do one or more of these behaviors.)
    Recorder: Indicate in COMMENT column the specific behavior(s).

2. Cries
    The child is tearful, fussing, and/or cries softly or loudly.

3. Rejects or ignores contact
    The child pushes or hits a peer or adult when contacted; or he retreats from or ignores the contact.

4. Wants out
    The child verbally and/or physically resists, indicating he wants to leave the situation. He may knock on the wall or door, turn the door knob, call for his parent, say "out," or "no." He may throw a tantrum, or throw toys.

B. STAYS TO HIMSELF

1. Engages in self-stimulation
    The child may suck his thumb or fingers, play with his hair, rock his body, stroke or tap parts of his body, flap and wave his hands, bang his head, nod his head, or make sounds in repetitive patterns.
    Recorder: Indicate specific behavior(s) in COMMENT column.

2. Watches, looks
    The child remains quiet, actively watching other children or activities, but does not move out into the environment.

3. Vocalizes or talks
The child sings or talks to himself or a toy. He may make sounds in a pattern but not the repetitive, self-stimulating type.

4. Plays with toys
The child plays with toys by himself, even if he moves out into the environment.

C. MOVES TOWARDS ADULTS

1. Makes physical contact with adult
The child makes physical contact with the adult by leaning against him, stroking, or pulling on clothing. The child may indicate by action (verbal or non-verbal) that he wants to be held by adult, parent, teacher, therapist, or other.

2. Controls adult
The child tries to prevent the adult from leaving the room, keeps one particular adult in view at all times, cries or protests when that adult leaves him to be with another child or leaves the area. The child is demanding of adult attention and directive of adults. *Recorder:* Indicate specific behavior(s) used by child in attempting to control adults. Use COMMENT column.

3. Ignores request by adult
The child does not respond to an adult's request to do something, or to stop doing something.

4. Communicates with adult
Child communicates with the adult through a variety of sounds or words, or through gestures.
Recorder: Note in COMMENT if this communication is in response to contact initiated by teacher or other adult.

D. MOVES TOWARDS PEERS

1. The child reaches out or touches peer
The child reaches out to peer with hand(s) or foot (feet) and/or touches peer.

2. Aggressive toward peer

The child pushes, grabs, wrestles, hits, takes toy away, pushes toy or equipment against peer.

3. "Talks" to peer
    The child communicates with peer by vocalizing or with gestures.

4. Plays with peer
    The child plays side by side with another child. He may take turns or share a toy.
    Recorder: Note in COMMENT column when these behaviors are in response to contact initiated by a peer.

E. MOVES TOWARD MATERIALS

1. Ignores toys or materials
    The child shows no awareness of toys or materials at hand, or pays no attention to them.

2. Perserverative use of toys/materials
    Child may continually spin wheels on car but not otherwise use car; may carry a toy or object around with him continually; uses material in a repetitive, non-changing way.

3. Negative use of toys/materials
    The child may knock toys or materials off tables and cupboards. He may throw toys and materials and otherwise abuse them.

4. Uses toys/materials presented to him
    While the child does not himself select the toy or material, he is interested in and uses them when they are placed before him.

5. Selects toys or activities and becomes involved
    The child selects, on his own volition, a toy or activity. He is able to focus on the toy or activity (looks at material while he is using it). He remains at the task for a period of time.

F. OVERALL STATE OF CHILD

1. Withdrawn
    The child remains non-responsive to the environment.

2. Emotionally upset

The child may cry, scream, pout, fight, ask repeatedly for parent, or try to leave the situation.

Recorder: Indicate specific behaviors in COMMENT column.

3. Distractible, inattentive
   The child's attention continually wanders from one thing to another, with little evidence of interest or involvement.

4. Calm and attentive
   The child accepts the situation. He may or may not be an active participant but complies with teacher requests and accepts routines.

5. Actively and enthusiastically involved in the environment
   The child is actively involved with materials and activities and/or people. He responds enthusiastically to environment (laughs, vocalizes, gestures).

BIBLIOGRAPHY

Barrett, M., Hunt, V. and Jones, M. Behavioral growth of cerebral palsied children from group experience in a confined space. *Dev. Med. Child Neurol,* 1967, 9, 1, 50-58.

Barrett, M., Jones, M. The sensory story: A multi-sensory training procedure for toddlers. *Dev. Med. Child Neurol.,* 9, 4, 448-456.

Connor, F. P. Curriculum guidelines for infant programs: Report of the task force on curriculum for United Cerebral Palsy Association, Inc. Collaborative Infant Program (in preparation).

Cyrulik-Jacobs, A., Shapira, Y., Bisno, A., and Jones M. Application of an automated operant response procedure to the study of auditory perception and processing ability of neurologically impaired infants. *Dev. Med. Child Neurol.,* 1975.

Friedlander, B. The effects of speech identity, voice inflection, vocabulary, message redundancy on infants' selection of vocal reinforcement. *J. Experim. Child Psy.,* 1968, 6, 443-459.

Friedlander, B. Receptive language development in infancy: Issues and problems. *Merrill-Palmer Quart.,* 1970, 7, 16.

Haynes, U. *The first three years — Programming for atypical infants and their families.* New York: United Cerebral Palsy Association, 1974.

Jones, M., Wenner, W., Toczek, A., and Barrett, M. Pre-nursery school program for children with cerebral palsy. *J. Amer. Med. Women's Association,* 1962, 17, 9, 713-719.

Jones, M., Barrett, M., Olonoff, C. and Andersen, E. Two experiments in training handicapped children at nursery school. In P. Wolff and R. MacKeith (Eds.), *Planning for better learning,* (Clinics in Developmental Medicine No. 33). London: William Heinemann Medical Books Ltd., 1969.

Kafafian, H. *Report of pan pacific rehabilition meetings, Sydney, Australia.* Washington: Cybernetics Institute, 1972.

Kehr, K., Pool program, UCLA Pre-nursery 1973-74. In *The first three years — Programming for atypical infants and their families* (Part II). New York: United Cerebral Palsy Association, 1974.

Mueller, H. Feeding and pre-speech. In P. Pearson, (Ed.), *Physical therapy in developmental disabilities.* New York: Charles Thomas, 1973.

Posner, N. Groups for mothers of handicapped infants. In U. Haynes (Ed.), *The first three years, Part II.* New York: United Cerebral Palsy Association, Inc., 1974.

Rogers, M., Burke, M., Jones, M., Kopp, C. Socialization inventory for young children, (unpublished).

Saunders, H. Reply to American Society of Landscape Architects Foundation request for illustrations of outdoors facilities for handicapped people. Los Angeles: School Building Planning Division, Los Angeles Unified School District, 1972.

Taylor, M., and Taylor, J. Regarding theraplay (Fun House), 4920 Dixie Drive, San Diego, California 92107.

VISUAL AIDS

Films - *Who Am I?* — 16 mm

> Black and white, sound, 25 minutes, documentary of pre-nursery including special interventions: sensory story, confined space, fun house, pool program.

Film - *Feeding and Pre-Speech Evaluation and Training* — 16 mm

> Black and white, sound, 30 minutes: Helen Mueller demonstrates steps in evaluation and training.

Film - *Theraplay (Fun House)* — Super 8 mm

> Color, silent, 20 minutes

Film - *Equipment for Moderately to Severely Handicapped Children* — Super 8 mm

> Color, 40 minutes, Sony, silent, cassette tape to accompany

Video Tapes - ½ inch, black and white

> Learning Box, Cyber-go-round, Transdisciplinary Approach

Brochure (in preparation) - Equipment for use with moderate to severely Handicapped Children.

CHAPTER 9

Evaluating Program Effectiveness

Bettye M. Caldwell

Like everyone else, I have my own favorite story to tell about evaluation, which is an easy process to parody. In the spring of 1965, I was asked to serve as a member of what at that time was called the "Technical Advisory Committee for Evaluation for Head Start." This group was given the impossible task of supporting the claims of phrasemakers that Head Start would cure all the social ills prevalent in America at the time. I well remember my attendance at the first meeting of this committee; there was an air of excitement, if not confusion, in the room in which we met. As the discussion got under way, a consensus was reached almost immediately: that some machinery had to be set into motion to evaluate this marvelous program that was about to be launched. But the consensus was a troubled one, because assessment techniques that could be used by relatively untrained persons with nonreading children were almost nonexistent. So the discussion and the debate went on and on. One of the men on this committee sat rather silently through much of the discussion and reacted only occasionally to all the testimonials offered by the people who were suggesting that some kind of evaluation of Head Start was essential. Finally it was his turn, and in a slow and deliberate manner he offered the following admonitions:

BETTYE M. CALDWELL is a Professor of Elementary Education at the Unisity of Arkansas and Director of the Center for Early Development and Education in Little Rock, Arkansas. Among her major interests are infant education and the evaluation of programs for children.

Those of you who feel this thing should be evaluated want to make absolutely certain about one thing. You don't want to design any kind of evaluation that will show that Head Start does not do all the things we are claiming it will do.

At the time I was shocked and felt that the suggestion represented lack of integrity and, even worse, a threat to the optimism of the period. And at that time we all needed to be optimistic, as the task ahead was formidable. Although it does not seem possible, that little episode occurred back in 1965. Since then, I have either become more sophisticated or more corrupt about evaluation as I can now understand some of the wisdom contained in that recommendation: do not collect any data which would how that your program does not accomplish what you say it will accomplish. All of my remaining remarks will be directed in one way or another toward having you decide whether this seeming wisdom represents sophistication or corruption. Essentially, what I am going to recommend is: do indeed collect data to prove that you did the things you said you would do to accomplish what you hope to accomplish.

THE PURPOSE OF EVALUATION

Although we often tend to use the word "evaluation" when speaking of an individual (child or adult), the word should probably be reserved for consideration of *program effectiveness* rather than consideration of child progress or diagnosis. Its root has to do with "finding the value in," and it is hoped that we try to do this more in programs than in individuals. When we refer to the determination of effectiveness in individuals, it would probably be better to use terms such as *assessing* or *diagnosing.* But when we "look for the value" in a program, we do this as a means of making some type of decision—deciding about how and where to allocate resources, whether to encourage innovation or to recommend replication of existing programs, what kinds of services are most likely to benefit some group, etc. In making such decisions, we usually go through a series of steps such as these:

First, we have to be able to *identify and formulate* the decision to be made. For example, do we need educational programs for handicapped infants? Maybe not. Perhaps our communities are saturated with such programs. Perhaps we should concentrate our efforts on children older than three.

Next, we have to *collect* some information relevant to the decision.

For example, how many handicapped infants are there in a particular community or state? What types of handicaps are represented? Are there available personnel or resources for developing and operating such programs? Are funds obtainable?

Third, we have to *analyze* the results of the information we have obtained. This information might have come from a large-scale screening program, from questionnaires sent to clinics and private physicians, from census-type population samples, from estimates of personnel supplied by various professional organizations, or from inquiries sent to state and federal agencies or to private foundations. What did we learn?

Fourth, we must *arrive at a decision or* plan of action. Perhaps we decide to establish a pilot program for ten children that involves a half-day, five-day-a-week preschool; or perhaps we decide to offer a language stimulation program to hard-of-hearing toddlers; or perhaps we decide to try to reach a "high risk" segment of the population with a prevention program.

Whatever we decide, our fifth step is to *take action* to implement our decision. We start our program—with three years of funding if we are lucky, with five years if we are blessed.

Then very quickly we must take our sixth step—*evaluate.* By means of the evaluation, we hope to demonstrate what we have accomplished, to prove to any skeptics that we did indeed do what we set out to do, and then to extend our efforts outward and disseminate the results of our evaluation and a description of our program to other persons and groups. We may make a deliberate effort to persuade others to try our approach by preparing materials that describe its major components. Training may be offered to all who are interested in our "model." In the meantime, some of our energy will be reserved for attempts to guarantee our model's continued existence by establishing continuing relationships with other organizations that serve children and by working to ensure continued funding for our program. In these dissemination efforts, the "results" of our evaluation will receive prominent attention, for without the evidence offered in the form of evaluation data, the program developers may not be able to persuade others that what they have done is worth emulating.

The proof we have sought has usually been in the form of the results of collective individual assessments of the sort described by Simeonsson (see Chapter 3). In general, we have favored what he termed the "achievement assessment model," although, as he documented, we have branched out considerably toward functional and competency assessments. Thus, for the most part, we have moved immediately to what has come to be called *summative evaluation*—product or outcome scores that summarize the performance of participants in a program in such a way that program planners can conclude that the program did or did not accomplish its stated objectives. There are certain procedures that we customarily use to help us decide whether a summative evaluation was any good: Were child-

150

ren assigned on a random basis? Was there a control group or some kind of placebo procedure? Were the proper statistical tests applied? Was testing or assessment done blind? To refer to my opening anecdote, we could note that Head Start was almost wiped out by summative evaluations that were carried out prematurely, possibly ineptly, and maybe even irrelevantly (or at least irreverently).

FORMATIVE EVALUATION—THE FIRST ESSENTIAL

So much effort goes into the task of planning any program and getting it funded and locally approved that we can sometimes be caught by surprise when the moment actually arrives to open our doors. Or, once underway, the energies of the director and other staff members may be so consumed by details of program operation that there is little or no time for thinking about evaluation. Many things can happen while you are out garnering community support for your program, going around to national meetings telling everyone about what marvelous things you are doing, writing last year's progress report while trying to draw up a proposal for next year's grant, recruiting children and families, convincing other agencies you are not going to duplicate their services—and on and on. Or possibly very little is going on at all. The staff may get cold feet and urge extension of a two-week pre-service program into a two-month program. Your curriculum director and your occupational therapist may decide that they cannot work together and that their ideas about what to do with and for the children are diametrically opposed, even though you carefully interviewed and ran key ideas by everybody. The person you hired to do individual work with families may suddenly realize that groups are her thing and inform you that she will not make individual home visits. The building that was to have been remodeled by the first of July may not be habitable until November, by which time you are one-third of the way through your first year's budget.

These are not just fantasies; each one has been taken from events that have occurred in our program or in those operated by friends and associates. What I am trying to illustrate is the absolutely critical point that, long before we try to make any kind of summative evaluation based on outcome (or process) measures on the children and families with whom we work, we must engage in continuing evaluations of the extent to which we are indeed implementing our own ideas and translating those ideas into practice. The purpose of such an evaluation is a cybernetic one—to help us get and keep on target in relation to the action decision we have made. This process has come to be called *formative evaluation,* and, as a means of evaluating program effectiveness, it is probably more essential than summative evaluation. So if we go back to my formulation of the six steps involved in making educational decisions, this calls for an intermediate step between steps five and six—i.e., between the action taken to implement a decision and the evaluation of the effectiveness or appropriateness of the chosen plan of action. How like its written description is a program in its operation? Can you read about it, visit it, and identify a concordance? Or, after a visit, does the written description seem like science fiction?

If you will now relate these questions to my opening anecdote which dealt with the poor judgement of collecting data which would expose your possible failure to accomplish what you set out to accomplish, you will understand why I feel my changed reaction represents experience rather than a loss of integrity. If a program rushes to the state of summative evaluation and bypasses the formative evaluation stage, it is possible to draw a false inference about the reasons for apparent failure to achieve objectives. The most likely inference is one which says, "It didn't work." Instead, the correct interpretation should perhaps be, "It didn't happen." It is not fair or wise to evaluate "a program" in the abstract unless a concerted effort has been made to determine that the program indeed represented a reasonable operational model of the adopted action plan. In many respects, the best way to evaluate the effectiveness of an educational program for infants (or for individuals of any age) is to *sample* that program and try to determine how closely it approximates a description of the program's stated goals and philosophy.

Before going on to suggest some ways of conducting meaningful formative evaluations of program effectiveness, let me say that these two aspects of evaluation (formative and summative) are probably not as easily differentiated as implied by Scriven (1967) and by Bloom, Hastings, and Madaus (1971). How the children perform collectively at some penultimate or ultimate summative evaluation should indeed provide guidance to program designers and implementers; and possibly the (formative) discovery that a certain type of program simply can't get off the ground because of logistical problems (e.g., a daytime-only home visiting program for working mothers) can serve a definite decision-making function. Nonetheless, for discussion purposes, we can try to keep them separate.

A MODEL FOR FORMATIVE EVALUATIONS

Many program operators are timid about undertaking program evaluation because they have allowed themselves to be mystified about the process and because they have perhaps been persuaded that only persons who are evaluation and measurement experts should undertake the process. Consultation from experts is always helpful, but there are many seemingly humble measures that staff members can competently use themselves which will offer a great deal of useful information to those who must plan and make decisions for future program operation. This is true for both formative and summative evaluation, but it is perhaps most relevant for the process of formative evaluation.

Stedman's model of individual assessment (see Chapter 3) is equally well-suited to the task of program evaluation. You will recall that this model refers to program inputs, to processes (or input-output relationships), and to outputs. It is easy to think of the first step as valid for formative evaluation, but we might immediately think that anything which is an output or which involves an input-output relationship is of a summative nature. Many outputs of a program, however, provide cybernetic rather than conceptual information, and, to the extent that they do, they should be considered as components of formative evaluation. In the remainder of this paper, we shall consider readily available sources of information which can be utilized by program staff for conducting the sort of formative evaluation of inputs, outputs, or input-output relationships upon which future program decisions can be based.

INPUTS

Program inputs refer to the components which ostensibly go into the operation of a program—its philosophy, the people who make it work, and the events which they arrange temporally and physically for all the persons who are to receive the service. Input evaluation is especially important in conducting formative evaluations, because without this step, we can never be sure what actually happened. A few examples of input evaluation follow:

> . . . What are the stated goals of the project? How realistic are these in relation to what is known about the characteristics of the handicapping condition present in the children to be served?

> . . . What types of staff members (disciplinary orientation, extent of training, cultural homogeneity or heterogeneity) have been hired to implement the program? Are there any gaps in the staff? Are there unnecessary duplications?

These variables were collected with the help of Craig Ramey (Inputs), Rune Simeonsson (Outputs), and Alice Honig (Input-Output Relationships) who led discussion groups at the 1975 TADS Conference on Infant Education.

... How much money is available to operate the program? What are the constraints on its use? What checks and balances are present to make certain that money is actually spent as intended?

... What is a typical day (sampled on some regular basis) like in the program? What actually happens to, for and with a child/parent unit on a sample of days?

... What is a typical staff day for different staff members? What do the people actually do with their time?

... How many staff members representing which professional and paraprofessionals left during a specified time period? What reasons were given for their leaving? How many were discharged? For what reasons?

... Are role descriptions available for each position, and are relationships between roles made explicit?

... What is the frequency and what are the types of interaction that this agency has with other agencies in the community?

... Is transportation provided? What happens to children while they are in transit?

... How is planning done? How often are the staff conferences held?

... What sort of pre-service and in-service training is provided?

... What are the stated goals of the clients being served? Is there consonance between clients, (e.g., parents) and project's goals?

... What sort of research is conducted as part of the project effort or by outsiders having a cooperative relationship with project staff? How is information from this research used to help clients or to guide program operation?

Obviously the articulation of varieties of inputs that can be used in a formative evaluation will vary with the nature of the project, the ages and types of handicapping condition of the clients, and with the skills and interests of the available staff. The input variables included in this list, however, should have wide applicability for any group offering early childhood services to families in which there is a young handicapped child.

OUTPUT VARIABLES

Output variables refer to accomplishments of a project, to outcomes which presumably relate in some way to the available inputs. Again it should be stated that in summative evaluation we are also interested in outputs. In order to serve a formative purpose, however, the measured output need not be a measured change within the individuals we are serving in the program nor even an outcome likely to persist for a long time. In fact, if formative evaluation is to accomplish its purposes, the output variables ought to have a certain transiency—i.e., since they should bear a relationship to inputs, and since inputs change, outputs useful for formative evaluation should be able to show change quickly. Some potentially useful output measures are as follows;

... How many children/families were served in a given time period (month, year)? How closely did this figure correspond to the estimated number?

... How many of what types of treatment were given? (How many physicals, occupational therapy sessions, home visits, parent group programs, field trips, etc.?)

... How many appointments were missed? For which type of service was the missed-appointment figure greatest? What follow-up was made of missed appointments? What reasons were given?

... How many people withdrew from the program? What reasons were given?

... How much money (if any) was earned toward the cost of the service?

... How many persons representing how many agencies visited the project within a specified time period?

... What kinds of staff training were offered? (How many sessions? What were the topics?)

... How many staff members resigned?

. . . How many referrals for service did the organization receive from other community agencies? What types of services were requested?

. . . What was the average length of time from date of first contact to initiation of service for clients?

. . . How many consultations to other community agencies (local, state, national) did staff provide during the year?

. . . How many families needing the type of service provided by the program were identified in a given period of time?

. . . How many volunteers, upon learning about the facility, provided services to handicapped children during the year?

. . . How many speeches did staff members give to local, state, and national organizations? How many papers were published?

Measurement of these output variables often involves only a simple count of some sort, or the calculation of a time interval. It should be commented that counting as a discrete type of evaluation is not likely to be productive unless the frequencies recorded can be related to specific program objectives. In the examples a year is often mentioned as the appropriate time interval for calculating the output variables. However, many of them can be used to monitor ongoing program activities and will be more useful for cybernetic functions if they are made frequently to determine how closely the project is approximating its stated goals.

Obviously the relevant output variables will differ from project to project. One type of facility would be meeting program objectives by receiving large numbers of referrals from existing agencies, whereas frequency of referral might be totally unrelated to the goals of other programs. Finally, a comment should be made that some of the output variables listed might also be considered as input. For example, the item relating to the number of staff members who resigned during a particular time period communicates something important about staff satisfaction. This seemingly subjective variable has clear components of both input and output. If the ratio of resigned to remaining staff members is high, this identifies a tense atmosphere which has to be considered part of the program input. On the other hand, it also communicates something about how successfully the program meets the needs of the adults who are participating in the venture and, as such, should be considered an output variable.

INPUT-OUTPUT RELATIONSHIPS

At the summative level, the input-output relationship will probably deal with broad groups of variables on the input side and with presumably lasting change within the children and parents for whom a program is operated on the output side. For summative evaluation in some cases, neither the input nor the output variables are subdivided at all—e.g., studies dealing with "the effect" (as measured by something like IQ) of "preschool education" (as defined by whatever occurred in the preschool in question) on retarded children. During previous years, when we were less sophisticated about evaluation, we might have tried to refine our analysis by dividing up at least our output variables by looking at "effects" (as measured by IQ, school achievement, absence of symptoms of emotional disturbance, etc.) of our still singularly defined input variable—i.e., preschool education. As we have gained new insights about the evaluation process, we have learned to break apart both our input and output variables in order to examine the relationships between them. Such division is especially important when we are doing formative evaluations. A few examples of useful types of input-output relationships for formative program evaluations follow:

... What is the relationship between temporary outcome measures such as the regularity of participation, verbal endorsement of program, expressed satisfaction with program, and utilization of different components of program (such as parent services only, child services only, parent and child services)?

... What is the relationship between flexibility of program delivery pattern (e.g., evenings, weekends, etc.) and participation by both fathers and mothers as opposed to mothers only?

... What is the relationship between frequency of contact and parental awareness of program goals?

... What is the relationship between frequency of parent contact with program components and diffusion of project ideas to other adults having contact with the target child (e.g., grandparents, baby-sitters, etc.)?

... What is the relationship between child's participation in the intervention program and mother's self-image as reflected in such variables as housekeeping, attention to other children in the family, social interactions with other families, and relations to community agencies?

... What is the relationship between child's participation in the program and parents' ability to serve as a child advocate when the child goes into a public school program?

... Is there a relation between providing transportation, baby-sitting for other children, not in the program, and increased family participation in the program?

... If a program does *not* offer a service necessary for achievement of one or more program objectives, are parents able to use their own ingenuity?

... What kinds of in-service training knowledge and skills are encountered by staff in relation to their own requests for training? What level of satisfaction do they have with the training that is provided?

... What is the "goodness of fit" between parent and/or child response and staff training?

... What is the frequency of different types of child behavior (crying, on-task behavior, aggression, smiling, singing) in different types of program activities?

... What is the relationship between frequency of participation and rate of change (motor, cognitive, affective) shown by the child?

Perhaps only the last of these examples needs any amplification, and that's because the inclusion of within-child variables makes it sound like summative evaluation. Changes in the children in these important areas of development do indeed represent summative evaluation. However, the changes can also be used for formative evaluation that is clearly related to important program decisions, such as how finances are expended. For example, if rate of change is as positive when participation of child and/or family is limited to two or three contacts per week as it is with five contacts, then the program model might be modified in such a way as to serve more children for shorter periods of time. Thus, more children and families are reached with no increase in expenditure. On the other hand, if no "positive" changes occur with less than a five-day program, decisions can be made about allocation of resources to fit this "fact" rather than to fit a set of hypothesized facts.

Essentially all these suggestions of ways of conducting formative evaluations involving input-output relationships call for the development and use of measures that are *not* reliable but that are sensitive to change. In general, educators have been trained to work toward the development of measures that are resistant to the effects of fluctuations in feelings, and attitudes. But the whole process for formative evaluation requires willingness to use some instruments that can give us differential feedback—feedback that is directly related to aspects of the program that are relevant to whatever decision we have to make.

SUMMARY

The importance of developing creative ways to launch formative evaluations of our own programs before we submit summative or pseudo-summative evaluations to our granting agencies, our colleagues, or the newspaper (or the *Congressional Record)* cannot be over emphasized. As formative evaluation involves having us look at ourselves rather than clients, we are not likely to be too comfortable in carrying out this type of activity. It is rather like laundering dirty linen in public. We might not like what we see if we look at ourselves as closely as we look at our children when we test them, interview them, weigh and measure them, and so on.

For the formative evaluation process we should not be afraid or ashamed to use seemingly unglamorous measures—unobtrusive measures, changeable rather than presumably highly reliable (time-stable) techniques, simple enumeration, and counting. Also we must remember to make certain that we sample all domains in which we have any objectives (cognitive, motor, affective) and that we sample all people whose lives are likely to be affected by our programs (children, parents, *staff).* Finally, we need to be aware that the first and most fundamental step in evaluating program *effectiveness* is to evaluate program *fidelity.* Only when we have this information should we go on to try to ask the questions, "What have our children learned?" and "How have they developed?"

RECOMMENDED READINGS

Popham, W. *An evaluation guidebook.* Los Angeles: The Instructional Objectives Exchange, 1972.

Stufflebeam, D., Foley, W., Gephart, W., Guba, E., Hammond, R., Merriman, R., and Provus, M. *Educational evaluation and decision making.* Itasca, Illinois: Peacock, 1971.

Tyler, R., and Wolf, R. (Eds.). *Crucial issues in testing.* Berkeley, California: McCutchan Publishing Corp., 1974.

Weinberg, R., and Moore, S. (Eds.). *Evaluation of educational programs for young children.* Washington, D.C.: Child Development Associates Consortium, 1976.

BIBLIOGRAPHY

Bloom, B., Hastings, J. and Madaus, G. (Eds.). *Handbook on formative and summative evaluation of student learning.* New York: McGraw-Hill, 1971.

Scriven, M. The methodology of evaluation. In *Perspectives of curriculum evaluation.* AERA Monograph on Curriculum Evaluation, No. 1. Chicago: Rand-McNally, 1967.

Index

Abecedarian Project, *see* Carolina Abecedarian Project
Abused children (battered children), 16
  assessing development of, 40
Achievement, assessing infant, 28-30
Achievement scales, advantages and limitations of, 30-32, 38
Achievement tests, 10
Adopted infants, assessing development of, 40
Age of entry, gains regardless of, 3-4
Albert Einstein Scale of Sensory-Motor Intelligence, 34-35
Alinsky, Saul, 83
Amblyopia, defined, 18
APPROACH interaction coding system, 97
Assessing the Behaviors of Caregivers (ABC; checklist), 97
Assessment
  effects of continued, 12
  inadequacy of methods used, 5-6
  See also Infant assessment
Attrition, problems of, 9
Autism, 16; *see also* UCLA Infant Intervention Program
Autonomous Achievement Striving Scale, 96

Badger, Earladeen, 45-62
Barrett, M., 133
Bayley, N., 30
Bayley Infant Behavior Record, 96
Bayley Scales of Infant Development, 30, 31, 39, 57-59
Beller, 96
Birth through one year of age, screening for eye disorders at, 19
Bloom, B., 151
Boehm Test of Basic Concepts, 95
Brazelton, T. B., 39
British Infant School, 83, 85
Bronfenbrenner, Urie, 4

Caldwell, Bettye, 81, 92, 96, 97, 145-59
Caldwell Preschool Inventory, 95
Camp, B. W., 30
Carey, W. B. A., 40
Carolina Abecedarian Project, 101-21
  evaluation and research within, 120

future plans for, 120-21
history and description of, 101-6
parent involvement in, 114-15
staff development in, 115-20
teaching-learning format in, 109-14
theoretical rationale for, 106-9
Carolina Infant Curriculum, 107-9, 116-17, 120, 121
Cattell Infant Intelligence Scale, 30, 31, 73, 95
Cerebral palsy, 40; *see also* UCLA Infant Intervention Program
Checklists
  Assessing the Behavior of Caregivers, 97
  Classroom Behavior, 96
  Hearing, 24-25
Child development trainers (CDTs), 90-92
Children's Center, *see* Family Development Research Program
Cincinnati Maternal and Infant Care Project, 45, 50, 56
Classroom Behavior Checklist, 96
Classroom Behavior Inventory, 96
Classroom Language Observation Checklist (CLOC), 95
Cognitive development in Family Rehabilitation Program, 71, 76-77
Cognitive use of language, 71
Collaborative Infants Project, 124
Collier, Albert M., 101-45
Competency model of infant assessment, 34-37
Confined space activity in UCLA Infant Intervention Program, 133
Confrontation used in Infant Stimulation/Mother Training Program, 49
Conry, J., 64
Contextualization in infant assessment, 39
Control groups, inadequacy of, 7
Corman, H. H., 34, 36
Cornell Descriptive Record of Infant Activity, 96
Criterion-reference tests, 10
Cultural differences, reactions to programs and, 6
Cultural-Familial Mentally Retarded (CFMR), *see* Carolina Abecedarian

Project; Family Development Research Program; Family Rehabilitation Program
Culturally deprived, defined, 9
Curriculum
  Carolina Infant, 107-9, 116-17, 120, 121
  FDRP, 82-84
  in Family Rehabilitation Program, 70-72
  See also Teaching-learning format
Cyber-Go-Round, 132
Cyruble-Jacobs, A., 132

Data processing, problems of, 8
Deaf/blind children, see UCLA Infant Intervention Program
Delayed effects of intervention programs, 11
Demonstration, teaching through, in Infant Stimulation/Mother Training Program, 49
Denver Developmental Screening Test (DDST), 30, 138
Development of Language (booklet), 48
Developmental achievements
  in Family Rehabilitation Program, 72-78
  in FDRP, 95
Development handicaps, see Infant assessment
Developmental problems, screening, diagnosis and treatment of, 20-22
Developmental Screening Inventory (DSI), 21
Developmental Screening Inventory (DSI) Questionnaire, 21
Dever, R., 64
Dewey, John, 83
Diagnosis
  assessment vs., 28
  of eye disorders, 18-20
  of hearing disorders and middle ear disease, 16-18
  of developmental problems, 20-22
Diagnosis and Treatment Program (EPSDT), 22, 23
Dismissal time in UCLA program, 131
Doll, E. A., 30
Down's Syndrome, 14; see also UCLA Infant Intervention Program
Duration recording, 32, 33

Early childhood intervention programs, 1-12
  problems with present, 5-12
  support for, 2-5
Early Language Assessment Scale (ELAS), 95
Eating time
  in Abecedarian Project, 112-14
  in UCLA program, 130
Education
  Family Style, 85-90
  See also Curriculum; Teachers
Eighteen-month to five-year old children in FDRP, 85-90
Emotionally disturbed infants, assessing development of, 40
Environmental changes, effects of, 8
Erikson, Erik, 83
Escalona, S. K., 34, 36
Ethical restrictions, 8
Evaluation
  of Abecederian Project, 120
  of FDRP, 94-97
  of Infant Stimulation/Mother Training Project, 57-60
  of UCLA program, 137-39
  See also Program effectiveness evaluation
Expressive area in Family Style program, 86
Eye disorders, screening, diagnosis and treatment of, 18-20

Family Data Record (FDR), 96
Family Development Research Program (FDRP), 81-99
  evaluation of, 94-97
  future plans for, 97-98
  goals and objectives of, 82-83
  measures used in, 96-97
  nature of parental involvement in, 90-92
  staff development for, 92-94
  teaching-learning format in, 84-90
Family Rehabilitation Program, 63-79
  developmental achievements in, 72-78
  infant stimulation project of, 68-72
  maternal rehabilitation program in, 66-68
  project design, 65-66
Family Style education in FDRP, 85-90
Family support services provided by Abecedarian Project, 104

FDRP, *see* Family Development Research Program
Feeding training in UCLA program, 131
Fifteen- to eighteen-month olds in FDRP, 85
Flynn, M., 75
Focus of programs, 11
Formative evaluation, 150-52
  model for, 151-52
Foster care, assessing development of infants in, 40
Frank Porter Graham Child Development Center (FPG), 101-2, 105, 106, 108
Frankenburg, William K., 13-25, 30
Frequency recording, 32, 33
Functional approach to infant assessment, 32-34

Garber, Howard L., 63-79
Gesell Developmental Schedules, 72, 74
Gesell examinations, 21
Gesell Scale, 30, 139
Gordon, Ira, 90
Grammatical Comprehension Test, 74, 75
Gray, S., 73
Griffiths, R., 30
Griffith's Mental Developmental Scale, 30, 31
Group pressure, inadequate maternal behavior altered by, 49
Groupings, *see* Multi-age groupings
Guide to Screening EPSDT Medicaid, 17

Hall, J. S., 112, 117
Hall, R. V., 32
Handicapped children
  in FDRP, 89
  rationale for early detection of, 13-16
  See also Infant assessment; Screening; UCLA Infant Intervention Program; *and other specific programs*
Harrington, Susan, 70, 71
Hastings, J., 151
Head Start, 22, 147, 150
Hearing disorders
  screening checklist, 24-25
  screening, diagnosis and treatment of, 16-18
Heber, Rick, 63, 64, 75, 76
Hess, R., 76
High Risk Index, 103
High-Risk Population Laboratory, 64

Hirschberg test (corneal light reflex test), 19
Hoffman, Caroline, 70, 71
Holmberg, Margaret C., 101-45
Home-based intervention programs, 2, 134
Honig, Alice S., 81-99
"How Babies Learn" (film; Caldwell), 92
"How Teacher Talk Creates Child Chatter" (Holmberg, Hall and Passey), 117
Human behavior, inadequate or naive theory of, 11
Hunt, J. McV., 34

Ill child care provided by Abecedarian Project, 106
Illinois Test of Psycholinguistic Abilities (ITPA), 72, 74-76, 95
Implicit Parental Learning Theory (IPLET), 96
Individualization of programs, need for, 6
Infancy period, educational program of Family Rehabilitation Program in, 71; *see also specific age groups*
Infant assessment, 27-44
  assessing achievement, 28-30
  approaches to, reviewed, 37-38
  competency model of, 34-37
  framework for, 38
  functional approach to, 32-34
  pertinent variables in, 38-39
  problems of special populations, 39-40
  suggestions for, 40-42
  typical scales used for, 30-32
Infant behavior model, 28, 29
Infant Behavior Record, 40
Infant Behavior Survey, 40
Infant Psychological Developmental Scale (IPDS), 34
Infant stimulation project in Family Rehabilitation Program, 68-72
Infant Stimulation/Mother Training Project, 45-62
  administrative considerations in, 56
  evaluation of, 57-60
  future plans for, 60-61
  goals and objectives of, 47-48
  history of and description of present, 45-47
  nature of parental involvement in, 55
  staff development for, 55-56
  teaching-learning format in, 48-54

Interval recording, 32, 33
Inventory of Home Stimulation (STIM), 96
IQ (intelligence quotient), 4-5, 7
  entry level, and benefits derived from intervention programs, 2
  in FDRP, 95
  in Family Rehabilitation Program, 73
  limitations of, 6, 10, 74
  See also Maternal IQ

Jones, M. H., 123-45
Jones, N.H., 32
Journal of American Medical Women's Association, 139
Juice time in UCLA program, 128-29

Kafafian, H., 132
Kehr, R., 132
Klaus, R., 73
Korner, A. F., 39

Laboratory tests to diagnosis developmental problems, 22
Lally, J. Ronald, 82, 83, 98
Language development
  in FDRP, 95
  in Family Rehabilitation Program, 71, 76-77
Language emergent years, 3
Large muscle area in Family Style program, 86, 88
Lay, Margaret, 82
Learning box, 132-33
"Learning to Learn in Infancy" (film; Stone), 92
LeLaurin, K., 112
Less-than-three-year olds, see UCLA Infant Intervention Program
Low socio-economic status (SES), mental retardation and, 63-64, 77
Lunch time in UCLA program, 130

Madaus, G., 151
Martin, H., 40
Maternal IQ
  in Abecedarian Project, 103, 104
  in Family Rehabilitation Program, 64-66, 76
Maternal rehabilitation program, 66-68
Measuring instruments, failure to develop appropriate, 10; see also specific scales and tests
Medical assessment in FDRP, 96

Medical care provided by Abecedarian Project, 105
Medical personnel in UCLA program, 135
Mental retardation, see Family Rehabilitation Program
Middle ear disease, screening, diagnosis and treatment of, 16-18
Milwaukee Project, see Family Rehabilitation Program
Morphology tests, 74
Mother/child interaction groups format for, in UCLA program, 133-34
Mother, see Infant Stimulation/Mother Training Project; Parental involvement; Parents; and specific programs
Mother's Guide to Early Learning (booklet), 48
Mueller, Helen, 131
Multi-age groupings
  in Abecedarian Project, 111-12
  in FDRP, 85-90
Muscle imbalance, ocular, 19

Nap time
  in Abecedarian Project, 112-14
  in UCLA program, 130-31
Neonatal Behavioral Assessment Scale, 39
Neuromuscular disorders, assessing infants with, 40
Newborns, screening, for hearing disorders and middle ear disease, 17
Nicholson, J., 40
Nutritional supplements provided by Abecedarian Project, 104

Observation, effects of continued, 12
Observation Scales of Personal Social Constructs, 96
One-year olds in Abecedarian Project, 110-11
Oral-pharyngeal development, 131
Orthopedists in UCLA program, 135
Outdoor play time in UCLA program, 129-30

Parent Evaluation of Program and Prognosis for Educational Responsibility (PEPPER), 96-97
Parental involvement
  in Abecedarian Project, 114-15
  in FDRP, 90-92

in Infant Stimulation/Mother Training Project, 55
in UCLA program, 134
Parents
and success of early childhood intervention programs, 2
in UCLA program, 139
Parmelee, A. H., 139
Payment for participation in Abecedarian Project, 104
Peabody Language Development Kit, 71
Personal development in Family Rehabilitation Program, 72
Phillips, J. L., Jr., 35
Physical plant of Family Rehabilitation Program, 68-69
Piaget, Jean, 34, 35, 42, 83, 107
Piagetian scales, 95
Piagetian theory, 34, 35, 38, 83
Play time in UCLA program, 127-30
Play test, 132
Pool activities in UCLA program, 131-32
Population
in Abecedarian Project, 102-5
interpreting nature of, 9
Posner, N., 124
Postural limitations, assessing development of infants with, 40
Preschool children, educational program of Family Rehabilitation Program for, 71-72; see also specific age groups
Prescreening Developmental Questionnaire (PDQ), 21
Prescriptive teaching, defined, 70
Pre-walking infants in Abecedarian Project, 110
Program effectiveness evaluation, 147-59
formative, 150-51
input-output relationships and, 156-58
model for formative, 151-52
output variables and, 154-55
program inputs and, 152-54
purpose of, 148-50
Psychiatrists in UCLA program, 135-36
Psycholinguistic quotient (PQ), obtained in Family Rehabilitation Program, 75
Psychologists in UCLA program, 137

Race, gains derived from intervention programs and, 2, 4

Ramey, Craig T., 101-45
Rating Form, 96
Reading tests, as misnamed, 10
Reimers, J. A., 40
Revised Bayley Scale of Infant Development, 21
Reyes, E. V., 75
Ricciuti, Henry, 96
Richardson, Elliott, 1
Risley, T. R., 112
Rogers, M., 125
Routine
in Abecedarian Project, 112-14
of Infant Stimulation/Mother Training Project, 52
in UCLA program, 127-33

Scales used in infant assessment, 30-32; see also specific scales
Scarr-Salapatek, S., 30
Screening, 14-22
for developmental problems, 20-22
for eye disorders, 18-20
for hearing disorders and middle ear disease, 16-18
presumptive nature of, 15
where is screening done, 22
Screening Test of Young Children and Retardates (STYCAR), 19
Scriven, M., 151
Sense experience area in Family Style program, 86
Sensory stories, function of, 133
Sentence Repetition Test, 74, 75
Services provided by Abecedarian Project, 104-6
Sex factor, and gains derived from intervention programs, 2, 4
Sigel, I. E., 27, 39
Shipman, V., 76
Simeonsson, Rune J., 27-44
Six- to fifteen-month olds in Family Development Research Program, 84-85
Six- to twelve-month olds in Infant Stimulation/Mother Training Program, 53-54
Six- to twenty-four month olds, screening, for hearing disorders and middle ear disease, 17, 24-25
Small muscle area in Family Style program, 86
Snack area in Family Style program, 87

Social-emotional development in FDRP, 96
Social skills, development of, 87
Social workers in UCLA program, 137
Socialization Inventory, 140-43
Socio-cultural retardation, see Carolina Abecedarian Project; Family Development Research Program; Family Rehabilitation Program
Socio-economic status (SES)
  and benefits derived from intervention programs, 2
  mental retardation and low. 63-64, 77
Sparling, Joseph H., 101-45
Special programs in UCLA program, 131-33
Sprigle program, 89
Staff
  in Abecedarian Project, 118-19
  of Family Rehabilitation Program, 68-72
  need for continuity of, 8
  quality and motivation of, and success of intervention, 3
  in UCLA program, 134-37
Staff development
  in Abecedarian Project, 115-20
  in FDRP, 92-94
  in Infant Stimulation/Mother Training Program, 55-56
Stanford-Binet Test, 5, 21, 72, 73, 95
States, infant assessment and infancy, 38-39
Stedman, Donald J., 1-12, 28, 152
Stone, Joseph, 92
Stories, sensory, 133
Successful early childhood intervention programs, 3-5
Summative evaluation, defined, 149

Teachers
  in Abecedarian Project, 112
  criterion performance reached by, 8
  in FDRP, 97
  prescriptive teaching, 70
  teacher effect as problem, 7-8
  in UCLA program, 134-35
  See also Curriculum; Staff; Staff development
Teaching-Learning format
  in Abecedarian Project, 109-14
  in FDRP, 84-90

in Infant Stimulation/Mother Training Project, 48-54
  in UCLA program, 125-34
Testing procedures in early intervention programs, 8
Therapists in UCLA program, 137
Theraplay (fun house), 133
Thomas, A., 40
Three- to six-month olds in Infant Stimulation/Mother Training Program, 51-53
Three- (or four-) week to three-month olds in Infant Stimulation/Mother Training Program, 50-51
Three-year olds
  in Abecedarian Project, 110-11
  screening, for eye disorders, 19
  screening, for hearing disorders and middle ear disease, 18
Time sampling, 32, 33
Time variable in infant assessment, 39
Toilet training
  in Abecedarian Project, 112-14
  in UCLA program, 128
Transportation provided in Abecedarian Project, 104
Treatment
  of developmental problems, 20-22
  of eye disorders, 18-20
  of hearing disorders and middle ear disease, 16-18
  treatment drift as problem, 7
Twelve- to eighteen-month olds in Infant Stimulation/Mother Training Program, 54
Two-year olds
  in Abecedarian Project, 110-11
  screening, for eye disorders, 19
Tyler, Ralph, 107

UCLA Infant Intervention Program, 123-45
  administrative considerations in, 136-38
  evaluation of, 137-39
  future plans for, 139-40
  goals and objectives of, 124-25
  parental involvement in, 134
  staff in, 134-37
  teaching-learning format in, 125-34
Uzgiris, I., 34
Uzigiris-Hunt Infant Ordinal Scales of Psychological Development, 57

VanNatta, P. A., 30
Vineland Social Maturity Scale, 30, 31,
    139
Visual acuity, 19-20
    testing two- and three-year olds for, 19
Volunteers in UCLA program, 137

Wachs, T. D., 34, 37
Wechsler Adult Intelligence Scale
    (WAIS), 65

Wechsler Intelligence Scale for Children
    (WISC), 72
Wechsler Preschool and Primary Scale
    for Children (WPPSI), 72
Well child care provided by Abecedarian
    Project, 105-6
Wiegerink, R., 33, 41
Williams, M. L., 30
Wright, T., 40